872 .TERE 2

12094

THE PENGUIN CLASSICS

FOUNDER EDITOR (1944–64): E. V. RIEU

PRESENT EDITORS:
Betty Radice and Robert Baldick

L156

TERENCE

The Brothers and
other plays

TRANSLATED WITH AN INTRODUCTION
BY BETTY RADICE

PENGUIN BOOKS

Penguin Books Ltd, Harmondsworth, Middlesex, England
Penguin Books Inc., 3300 Clipper Mill Road, Baltimore 11, Md, U.S.A.
Penguin Books Pty Ltd, Ringwood, Victoria, Australia

—

This translation first published 1965

—

Copyright © Betty Radice, 1965

—

Application for permission to perform these
plays should be made to the League of Dramatists,
84 Drayton Gardens, London s.w.10.

—

Made and printed in Great Britain
by Richard Clay (The Chaucer Press), Ltd,
Bungay, Suffolk
Set in Monotype Bembo

CONTENTS

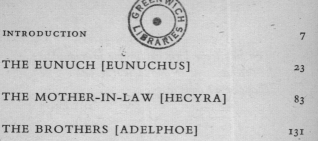

C'est une tâche bien hardie que la traduction de Térence: tout ce que la langue latine a de délicatesse est dans ce poète.

DIDEROT

INTRODUCTION

Comedy is a more intellectual and sophisticated art than tragedy, and on the stage it depends for its effects on verbal exchange. Its characters must be wholly articulate, and if it is to succeed it needs an equally articulate, civilized audience, who can respond not with hilarity so much as with a delighted amusement. Audiences of this kind evidently existed for comedy to flourish in fifth-century Athens, in Hellenistic Greece, in Elizabethan and Restoration England, in the Paris of Louis XIV, eighteenth-century Venice, and in Edwardian London, but Rome of the second century B.C. gave small encouragement to a young man who had all the requisites to make him a great writer of comedy. Terence died young, and could be judged a failure in his own day, but the originality he showed in his treatment of his Greek models had a lasting influence on the history of western drama. The six plays of Terence are his complete works. Attached to each play is an authentic prologue, a personal apologia of unique literary interest, and several of the medieval MSS. are headed by a production notice giving the date of composition and details of the first production. There is also a Life of Terence[1] by Suetonius with an addition by the grammarian Aelius Donatus, preserved with Donatus' very full commentaries on the plays. It would seem that a lot is known about Terence and his work; in fact he remains one of the most problematic of ancient authors, and there were conflicting accounts of him within a century of his death.

Tradition says that Publius Terentius Afer was born in Carthage in 185 B.C. (some say 195) of native Libyan stock,

and came to Rome as the slave of the senator Terentiu
Lucanus who gave him a good education and his freedom. H
was slight, dark, and good looking, and his abilities wor
him entry into the 'Scipionic circle' – the group of intellectua
young nobles gathered round Scipio Africanus the Younger
He made a good impression on the elderly dramatist Caecilius
to whom he read his first play, and so he embarked on hi
own stormy career. Though he won instant success witl
The Eunuch, *The Mother-in-Law* failed twice and only suc
ceeded at the third attempt through the loyal efforts of hi
actor–producer Ambivius Turpio. His association with th
Scipios led to slanderous rumours that his noble friends ha
helped him, or even written his plays for him, and he was fre
quently accused by an old playwright, Luscius Lanuvinus, o
plagiarizing earlier Latin plays and tampering with the Gree
models he professed to be translating. Soon after 160, in hi
twenty-fifth year, he left Italy in search of more Gree
comedies for adaptation, met with some accident in Greec
or Asia Minor, and never returned. By the time Suetoniu
wrote his *Life* at the end of the first century A.D. there were a
least four versions of his death and no agreement on whethe
he died rich or poor.

Amid so many conflicting views it is not surprising tha
scholars have argued that the *Life* is no more than inventio
based on the few facts that emerge from the plays themselve
the prologues, and the production notices. For example, th
connexion with the Scipio circle could have been conjecture
simply from the statement in the production notice to *Th
Brothers* that it was first performed at the funeral games o
Aemilius Paullus, Scipio's natural father. Even the surnam
Afer is no proof that Terence was of north African origin
witness the famous lawyer Domitius Afer. What is clear fror
the multiplicity of opinion quoted by Suetonius is that th

Romans themselves were always puzzled by Terence's brief career and sudden end.

There is no doubt that Terence did have 'noble friends', for they are mentioned in the prologues, where he glories in his association with 'men whose services in peace, in war, and in your private affairs are given at the right moment, without ostentation, to benefit each one of you' (*The Brothers*, 19–21). The suggestion that they helped him with his plays lingered on, to be referred to by Cicero in a letter to Atticus (7.3.10) and much later by Quintilian, though with reserve (*Institutio Oratoris*, 10.1.99). But if Scipio or any of his friends wrote the plays, it is surprising that no more of the same type were written after Terence's early death. Internal evidence from the plays themselves points to more indirect influence. The lively farcical element which made Plautus deservedly popular is absent; instead Terence provides subtlety of plot, development of character, and economy of dialogue, which imply an attentive, educated audience ready to appreciate the finer points of a Hellenistic comedy presented in the most lucid and elegant Latin which had yet been written. *The Mother-in-Law* is not a play likely to succeed on a large open-air stage before a crowd expecting the rollicking gaiety of Plautus, and consequently only too ready to slip off to see the gladiators and tight-rope walkers; but is it too fanciful to imagine its being performed in the house of a cultivated aristocrat to an invited audience of his friends?

Publius Cornelius Scipio Aemilianus Africanus Numantinus Minor was the son of Lucius Aemilius Paullus, the victor over the Greeks at the battle of Pydna which ended the Third Macedonian War. As part of the spoils of war Paullus took the Greek library of King Perseus of Macedon and sent it home to Rome. Scipio had fought at Pydna and toured

Greece with his father; his early education on Greek lines is described by Plutarch in his life of Aemilius Paullus. Before 160 he was adopted by his cousin Lucius Cornelius Scipio, himself a writer and phil-Hellene, and in Rome he headed a group of young men with literary and philosophic interests, notably Lucius Furius Philus, Gaius Lucilius, the satirist admired by Horace, and Gaius Laelius, surnamed Sapiens for his Stoic inclinations. The philosopher Panaetius of Rhodes and the Greek historian Polybius were among their friends. Laelius and Scipio both appear in Cicero's *de Senectute*, and his *de Amicitia* commemorates their friendship. Furius Philus joins them in the discussion which forms the framework of *de Republica*, and this takes place in Scipio's garden in the winter sunshine. In *de Oratore* (2.6.22) there is the well-known account of Laelius and Scipio on a carefree holiday, picking up shells on the seashore, and Horace writes of Scipio, Laelius, and Lucilius 'fooling about till the cabbage was boiled' (*Satires*, 2.1.71); the scholiast caps this with a tale of Laelius' surprising Lucilius chasing Scipio round the dining-room with a knotted napkin. One can imagine these young men more ready to make a friend of someone of different race and social class than the 'men of consular rank' whom the grammarian Santra believed to have been Terence's patrons. On his side, 'by birth a Phoenician,[1] by intellectual education a Greek, by the associations of his daily life a foreigner living in Rome, Terence was more in sympathy with the cosmopolitan mode of thought and feeling which Greek culture was diffusing over the civilized world, than with the traditions of Roman austerity or the homely humours of Italian life.' This is what makes the difference between Terence and Plautus more than one of generation: 'The great gap which was never

1. i.e. Semitic; or he may have been a Berber (W. Y. Sellar, *Roman Poets of the Republic*, 1889).

again to be bridged over had been made between the mass of the people and a small educated class.'

Plautus died in 186 B.C., so that all his plays were first produced in the years of austerity at the end of the second Carthaginian war and the changed social conditions produced by the rapid increase of an urban and slave population. They were all taken from Greek New Comedy of Menander and his contemporaries, and military service must have brought many Romans in contact for the first time with the more sophisticated Greek cities of South Italy and Sicily; but Roman society was still parochial and puritanical, based on the close ties of family life. There was nothing in it to correspond with the *jeunesse dorée* of the Hellenistic world, young men in debt to pimps and mistresses, their elders worldly-wise, and their servants as resourceful as Figaro or Scapin. Consequently, Plautus was restricted to using stock types of character which sometimes approach caricature. He could not risk outraging Roman morality by humanizing them. Even so, the best of his plays are excellent theatre and genuinely entertaining, thanks to his native Italian wit, his flair for exploiting a situation and striking a balance between lively comedy and irreverent farce, and his verbal dexterity. His plays were also famous in their day for their songs and musical accompaniment, so perhaps they fall somewhere between *The Comedy of Errors* and *Orpheus in the Underworld*.

Terence's first play was produced nearly twenty years later. *The Woman of Andros* starts with a conversation between an Athenian gentleman and his trusted freedman. Their neighbour, a courtesan from Andros, has died; and her young sister's unaffected grief at the funeral has won general sympathy and made it impossible for her young lover to conceal his feelings, although he is about to be married to someone else. The dialogue form is Terence's own improvement on his

Greek model, and there is no formal prologue to give an advance solution to the problem posed. The tone is light but sympathetic, the language is direct and simple, and the whole scene has been beloved and quoted by critics from Cicero down to Sainte-Beuve, who compares some of its phrases with Andromache's smiling through her tears. The stage is set for the playwright who can give his Thais and Bacchis some of the warmth and humanity of Marguerite Gautier, and whose *Brothers* recalls Molière in its blend of irony and wit. These are plays written for a small cultivated audience by a young man alive to the requirements of plot and character, blessed with the gift of language to express a range of emotions, and unfettered by the conventions of an earlier age. It is not surprising that they met with instant criticism from older rivals, and understandable that, in comparison with Plautus, Terence was judged a half-sized Menander lacking in verve.

Roman comedy took over from Greek New Comedy its stage conventions, the back of the stage showing the doors to two or three houses, and the side entrances leading to the country on the spectators' left and the town centre on the right. All stage action took place in the open street, and the greater breadth of stage made it easier to accept the convention that characters on the stage heard only what the author intended them to hear. The style of acting was declamatory, with formalized gestures, costume was stereotyped, and actors were probably masked in the Greek fashion to indicate the typical characters listed in the prologue to *The Eunuch*: 'a running slave, virtuous wives and dishonest courtesans, greedy spongers and braggart soldiers.' In this rather unprepossessing framework Plautus created something much more vigorous and exuberant than his original, with characters speaking dialogue less detached and polished because it relects his own age; the down-to-earth realism belongs to his native Italy, while the gaiety and extravaganza is the product of Plautus' lively imagination. But Terence represents the leaven of the new Hellenism beginning to work, the more open-minded tolerance which was anathema to reactionaries such as the elder Cato. (It has been observed that 'the century after Cato is a period of prosaic nationalistic literature in which no man of real genius appears.'[1]) Terence also developed a form of Latin which can be as subtle and sensitive as the Greek of Menander. As Sainte-Beuve puts it, '*C'est le secret des âges polis. Térence est le premier chez les Romains qui " D'un mot mis en sa place enseigne le pouvoir".*'[2]

This was recognized by Roman critics, Cicero and Caesar (quoted by Suetonius), Horace and Quintilian. No other Roman writer except Horace was able to express himself so unaffectedly in a style quite untouched by the influence of rhetoric. Finally, any lack of high spirits in his comedies was more than compensated for by characters with greater depth, and situations rich in dramatic surprises where genuine problems were handled with sympathy and perception. This is what enabled Gilbert Norwood to call *The Mother-in-Law* 'the purest and most perfect example of classical high comedy strictly so-called which dramatic literature can offer from any age or nation'. The timeless quality of these comedies is due to Terence's sanity and perceptiveness, which could show people as basically the same then as now – mixed in their unconscious motives, muddled in their intentions, but, like the young men in *The Brothers*, good at heart. What is caricature in Plautus and satire in Juvenal is irony in Terence, a not unkindly commentary on the foibles and frailties of men.

Terence's adaptation of the prologue in order to answer his

---

1. Tenney Frank, *Life and Literature in the Roman Republic*, p. 21.
2. *Nouveaux Lundis*, 10 August 1863.

critics shows that he was a conscious artist who knew quite
well what he was trying to do. He was accused of writing thin
dialogue, of stealing characters and scenes from earlier Latin
plays, of accepting unacknowledged help from his noble
patrons, and of tampering with his Greek originals to the
extent of picking and choosing from more than one for
each of his plays, thus rendering them useless to other transla-
tors. He never formally refutes the charges, but counter-
attacks. His critic, he says, is a competent translator with no
stage sense, and the question of plagiarism in his own work
does not arise; he has merely made use of the usual characters
and ignored what other playwrights have put on the stage.
'Nothing in fact is ever said which has not been said before'
(*The Eunuch*, 40–41). When he alters a Greek original it is for a
purpose: a new scene is fitted into *The Brothers*, and the soldier
and his hanger-on added to the original of *The Eunuch*, but a
new dramatic whole is created from which the additions could
not possibly be removed. Terence is really more an original
dramatist masquerading as an adaptor, and this may be why
no one else attempted anything of the same genre. There were
so many spurious Plautian plays that Varro had to establish a
canon of authentic ones. Terence remained 'caviare to the
general'.

A few names survive of other authors of *fabulae palliatae*
(plays in Greek dress) but the last is that of Turpilius, who died
as a very old man in 103 B.C. The *fabulae togatae* based on
native Italian themes lasted longer; the titles of more than
seventy plays are known and the names of three playwrights,
Titinius, Afranius, and Atta. But the uneducated city crowds
preferred the mimes, farces, and burlesques which 'split the
ears of the groundlings' and were to take over the stage entirely from true comedy. Nothing survives of these except
references such as Horace's tale of the Campanian buffoons in his

Satires (1.5.51 ff.), and the stock characters of Punch and Judy which have come down to us through the Commedia dell'Arte from the rustic Atellane farce. Any comedy written under the Empire was intended for reading aloud to an invited audience; Juvenal opens his first Satire with a protest against the tedium of these readings, and Pliny (*Letters*, 6.26) writes enthusiastically of a young friend's gifts as a playwright without any suggestion that these plays might be staged. It is significant that when Quintilian wishes to illustrate a comment on the acting of comedy he refers to Terence's *Eunuch* and nothing later. He implies that there were occasional revivals of the old comedies in the splendid Imperial theatres, but the *Incendium* of Afranius was revived only to give a stage spectacle of a fire (Suetonius, *Nero*, 11). Even as far back as Cicero and Horace, Terence was more quoted for his humanity and style than for his stagecraft. Similarly, Seneca's verse tragedies were never intended for stage performance.

When the barbarians closed in on Rome and Latin scholars took refuge in the monasteries, Terence was one of the authors whose works were carefully preserved complete. The earliest manuscript is the Codex Bembinus of the fourth or fifth century, containing all the plays with the exception of a large part of *Andria*. From the ninth century onwards, there are a large number of manuscripts stemming from a different source, which provide the production notices and a wealth of scribal correction (and error). Some are illustrated by drawings showing scenes from the plays.[1] They are quoted by a wide range of authors down to the sixth century, and the latest of the commentators working on them is the tenth-century Eugraphius. All this goes to show the loving care which scholars bestowed on Terence, whose Latin served as a

1. See M. Bieber, *The History of the Greek and Roman Theater*, 2nd ed. 1961, pp. 153–4.

model of clarity and style for people struggling to keep the classical language alive. As his plays had long since left the stage, they escaped the severe censure of the Fathers of the Church who rightly attacked the brutality and indecency of the mime and melodrama in the late Empire. We know that Terence was read and enjoyed from St Augustine and St Jerome, who complained that the ancient comedies could distract the devout from their bibles. In the tenth century, an aristocratic Saxon nun, Hrotsvitha of Gandersheim, even wrote plays on sacred subjects in the manner of Terence, in an attempt to purge him of his worldliness. One has only to dip into this literary curiosity to be aware of her appreciation of her model.[1]

With the coming of the Renaissance, the popular pageants and morality plays encouraged by the western Church gradually yielded to the discipline of classical tragedy and comedy, with Seneca, Plautus, and Terence as the greatest influence on European drama. In Italy the movement started with learned works in classical style like the *Philodoxius* of Alberti; then came actual performances of such plays, such as those sponsored in the Rome of Sixtus IV by the antiquarian Pomponius Laetus. Finally, the ancient dramatists reached a wider public through direct translation, with some of the great principalities of North Italy leading the way. In 1496 we find the Marquis of Mantua writing to his father-in-law, Hercules I of Ferrara, for copies of the plays of Plautus and Terence translated and played at Ferrara, and there are performances also recorded at Milan under Lodovico Il Moro. Ariosto is known to have translated *Andria* and *The Eunuch*. The presses of Venice produced both verse and prose translations of Terence and selections from Plautus; then original comedy began to be written in Italian, and by the mid sixteenth cen-

---

1. See Helen Waddell, *The Wandering Scholars*, 1934, ch. 3.

tury the movement was spreading over western Europe.
Spain provides one of the earliest examples of classical comedy
in de Rojas' dramatized novel, *La Celestina*,[1] and later in the
plays of Lope de Vega and his contemporaries. The first
English comedy, *Ralph Roister Doister*, written by Nicholas
Udall about 1553, is directly modelled on Plautus' *Braggart
Soldier* and Terence's *Eunuch*; but the best of the Elizabethan
comedies have an element of fantasy which is a distinguishing
mark of English comedy at its best and something quite alien
to the Latin–Italian style. Shakespeare realizes his powers in
comedy when he moves away from the formal pattern of *The
Two Gentlemen of Verona* and *The Comedy of Errors* towards
the greater poetic depth and freedom of *As You Like It*
and *Twelfth Night*. With the post-Restoration dramatists,
Wycherley, Vanbrugh, and, above all, Congreve, there is a
return to true classic comedy in a somewhat coarsened form;
to be followed in the next century by Goldsmith and Sheridan
writing with more polish in the same style. The greatest of
these plays, *The Way of the World*, is prefaced by Congreve's
personal tribute to Terence. But as Diderot pointed out, the
characters in English classic comedy tend to become cari-
catures; in his opinion there have been only two comic
dramatists with the gift of drawing characters in depth, with
sympathy and without exaggeration, placing them in situations
designed to reveal both their individuality and their timeless-
ness: Terence and Molière. The great writers of English
comedy have not written for the stage – they are among the
poets, essay-writers, and novelists, Chaucer, Addison, Fielding,
and Jane Austen.

Terence has had his most sympathetic admirers since the
seventeenth century in France, where his humanism and his
sense of style had greatest influence. This is apparent from the

1. Translated by J. M. Cohen as *The Spanish Bawd*, Penguin Classics, 1964.

tributes of critics such as Montaigne, Diderot, and Sainte-Beuve, but his true spiritual descendant is of course Molière. In Molière we find the true humanistic approach – sanity and common sense, freedom from cant and exaggerated sentiment, an understanding of the sufficiency of the world and man's part in it. He can use comedy as a medium for a sustained social commentary, and his essential seriousness can lift it to its highest level so that under the impact of laughter we are made to feel the truth of his judgement on us all. Terence may be limited by the convention that he must 'translate' light Greek comedy into a different world of thought and sentiment, but although he takes over the typical irascible father, irresponsible youth, courtesan, and slave-dealer, he too presents them as individuals caught up in a complicated situation involving human relationships. A complex plot has endless comic potentiality when characters are set at cross purposes and no one is in full possession of the truth until the denouement; while in the meantime the confusion reveals a great deal about the persons involved which would otherwise remain unknown. Terence does not moralize, but his attitude is basically moral, and his characters are never vicious, only self-deluded. A young man seduces a girl, but 'there were excuses . . . it is human nature'. Yet he is not allowed to shirk the consequences and leave her in the lurch. A strict father believes he is doing the best thing for his son; but if he makes no allowances for youth, he lives in a fool's paradise. A woman can be dismissed by her neighbours as a professional courtesan and later show true generosity and an almost maternal affection towards her former lover. Terence is as much the creator of Aeschinus, Demea, and Bacchis as Molière is of M. Jourdain and Célimène.

There is something elusive about comedy which makes it difficult to define, and that part of the *Art of Poetry* is lost where

Aristotle gave it full treatment. He left only a provisional distinction between tragedy and comedy, the one dealing with the fate of an individual and stirring the emotions, and the other depicting social groups and aiming at a sense of the ridiculous. The writer of comedy may point his finger at wrong ideas, as Shaw did, or at social pretensions and sentimental notions, like Congreve and Sheridan. He can be as brilliant as Wilde, as romantic as Synge, or as caustic as Maugham; his interest may be primarily in character, as Jonson in *Volpone*, or in intrigue of plot as in *Figaro*. But if he is not to write satire his handling of characters must be kindly, he must know people as they really are to avoid burlesque, and retain a sense of proportion to keep free of exaggeration and farce. He needs a natural optimism if his purpose is not sick comedy; as Meredith put it, 'To love Comedy you must know the real world, and know men and women well enough not to expect too much of them, though you may still hope for good.'[1] In his famous essay *On Books*, Montaigne wrote: 'As for Terence, who personifies the charm and grace of the Latin tongue, I am astounded by the lifelike way in which he depicts ways of thought and states of manners which are true of us today; at every turn our actions send me back to him.' This is still true, for, though the six plays are short and undeveloped by modern standards, each one expresses in a different way Terence's own much quoted principle: *Homo sum: humani nil a me alienum puto.* 'I am human myself, so I think every human affair is my concern.'

*

There have been several English translations of Terence, most of them the 'dry and literal interpretation of the text' which outraged Gibbon during his brief stay at Oxford. My attempt has been made both to bring out the excellent stage-

---

1. *An Essay on Comedy*, 1877.

craft of the comedies and to encourage those who can to go to the Latin and enjoy an author 'whose style can charm, whose every word delights'. The second headmaster of Westminster School after the suppression of the Abbey under Henry VIII 'brought in the reading of Terence for the better learning the pure Roman style', and it is our loss that later educationists confined young people to Roman history and oratory and Augustan poetry, to the neglect of the colloquial classical Latin which can be spoken trippingly, not rolled out like a rhetorical period. It does not need a very profound knowledge of Latin to enjoy an exchange like that of *Adelphoe*, 13 ff. (*The Brothers*, p. 156).

> DEMEA fit sedulo;
> nil praetermitto; consuefacio; denique
> inspicere, tamquam in speculum, in vitas omnium
> iubeo atque ex aliis sumere exemplum sibi:
> 'hoc facito.' SYRUS recte sane. DE. 'hoc fugito.' SY. callide.
> DE. 'hoc laudist.' SY. istaec res est. DE. 'hoc vitio datur.'
> SY. probissime. DE. porro autem . . . SY. non hercle otiumst
> nunc mi auscultandi. piscis ex sententia
> nactus sum: i mihi ne currumpantur cautiost.

In the early days of the old public schools it was common practice for the scholars to give regular performances of Roman comedies, but only Westminster School has remained faithful to Terence and its foundation statute of 1561 which said that every Christmas the school should present a Latin play. Between 1703 and 1938 the records are almost complete, and show that *Adelphoe*, *Andria*, and *Phormio* were played in rotation, with *Eunuchus* for a fourth until 1860 when it was replaced by Plautus' *Trinummus* and finally by *Rudens*. (Since the Latin play was revived it has been played in summer, in modern dress out-of-doors, with a freer range of choice from Plautus and Terence.) Whether in Latin or in translation, these plays are eminently actable, and as they need no elaborate scenery and have their stage directions built into the dialogue, the spoken word can make an immediate impact on the listener.

Terence was of course a poet as well as a dramatist, though a less inventive craftsman in words than Plautus. He wrote for the most part in six-foot iambic verse, with variations in trochaic feet for excitable talk. Latin poetry in his day had not yet adopted the strict rules of quantity taken over from the Greek poets, and scansion was determined more by ear, the accent falling more or less in line with that of natural speech. The nearest English equivalent to this would be blank verse; but prose has always been the medium for English comedy where the emphasis is on wit and the nimble thrust and parry of dialogue. Shakespeare's prose passages in *Much Ado* and *As You Like It* are striking evidence of this. I have therefore made no attempt to reproduce Terence's verse, hoping that prose would express more naturally both the lucidity of his argument and the direct simplicity of his language.

The division of Roman plays into five acts, which became the strict five-act law of post-renaissance drama, was probably based on a misunderstanding of Horace's *Ars Poetica* (189-90) which gives that as a practical guide for the length of a play, the sections to be marked by suitable choral interludes. But no trace of such interludes exists in Terence's plays, and the act division of the MSS. is not his. Indeed, Donatus remarks that *The Eunuch* was played continuously for fear bored spectators left their seats, and some of the prologues in Plautus indicate that a long non-stop performance was about to begin. I have therefore removed the conventional act divisions, and indicated only where the progress of the play demands a short interval. The early MSS. mark the entry and exit of a character by a scene number; I have changed this to a more usual indication, and have added the minimum of stage directions for easy reading of the plays. The translation follows the Oxford text of Kauer and Lindsay, with help from that of J. Marouzeau in the French Budé series. Three plays have been chosen for this volume to illustrate different aspects of Terence's work, and the remaining three will follow in a second volume. I am grateful to all my friends who have shown a helpful interest in the plays, from the Founder Editor of the Penguin Classics down to some of my old pupils at Channing School, and in particular to Mr E. F. Watling, who has never begrudged time and trouble spent on reading my work and suggesting how it could be improved.

Highgate 1964　　　　　　　　　　　　　　　　　　B. R.

The Eunuch

[EUNUCHUS]

INTRODUCTORY NOTE

The Eunuch is Terence's second play, and the one which brought him most success in his lifetime. It shows Terence already at work as an innovator, adapting the scene where Chaerea tells his tale from monologue to dialogue, and introducing the soldier and his hanger-on from another Greek model to be skilfully integrated into the plot. It is the most Plautian play he wrote, light-hearted and lively, and, though none of the characters is very subtly conceived, the light touch is consistent and dramatically right. Thais is a courtesan, but that is a matter of social status rather than morals, and she has charm and personality in marked contrast with the conventional views expressed about her profession. Pythias' gift for repartee makes her much more than a stock maidservant, and she is given an excellent scene where she pricks Parmeno's bubble of self-satisfaction. The awkward young countryman Chremes is artfully drawn as a foil to the more sophisticated brothers, Phaedria and the ebullient young Chaerea, who is the prototype perhaps for Beaumarchais' Cherubin. The inherent improbabilities in the play (too little time is allowed for Chaerea's escapade, and Chremes sobers up remarkably quickly) escape notice in the rapid development of surprises. Inevitably *The Eunuch* has been criticized for its a-moral handling of Chaerea's conduct and the heartless solution of the rivalry between Phaedria and Thraso, but this is a comedy essentially aimed at amusing its audience. Robert Graves has even suggested that *The Eunuch* could be 'recast as a modern musical with great success'.

PRODUCTION NOTICE

THE EUNUCH by Terence: performed at the Megalesian Games[1] during the curule aedileship of Lucius Postumius Albinus and Lucius Cornelius Merula.

Produced by Lucius Ambivius Turpio and Lucius Atilius of Praeneste.

Music composed by Flaccus, slave of Claudius, for two right-hand[2] pipes.

Greek original by Menander.

The author's second play, written during the consulship of Marcus Valerius and Gaius Fannius.[3]

1. Celebrated annually on 4 April in honour of the Great Mother, the goddess Cybele.
2. Two pipes could be played, one by each hand; this was probably the treble pipe.
3. i.e. 161 B.C.

SYNOPSIS[1]

A girl was wrongly said to be the sister of Thais; unaware of this, the soldier Thraso brought her with him as a present for Thais. In fact, she is a freeborn Athenian. Thais' lover, Phaedria, gives orders for a eunuch he has bought to be given to her, is persuaded to yield his place to Thraso for two days, and departs for the country. Phaedria's young brother is desperately in love with the girl given to Thais; on Parmeno's suggestion he dresses up as the eunuch, gains admission to the house, and seduces the girl. But an Athenian citizen is found to be her brother and gives her in marriage to her seducer. Thraso comes to terms with Phaedria.

1. Each of Terence's six plays has a synopsis written in the mid second century A.D. by Gaius Sulpicius Apollinaris of Carthage.

If people exist who try to please as many and hurt as few honest men as possible, the author begs to announce himself one of their number.

Furthermore, if someone has thought something too harsh has been said against him, he must realize that this was not an attack but an answer. He gave provocation first when for all his clever translation his poor workmanship turned good Greek plays into bad Latin ones. He[1] is the man who has just given us *The Spectre* of Menander, and in his *Treasure* puts the defendant's explanation of his claim to the money before the plaintiff states his case and says how he came by the treasure and how it found its way into his father's tomb. Do not let him deceive himself or fancy that once he retires I shall have no more to say: he is wrong, and I warn him not to provoke me further. There are plenty of other things I am overlooking for the moment which I can produce later on if he continues to attack me as he set out to do.

The play we shall present today is *The Eunuch* of Menander. After the aediles had bought it, he managed to be present at a rehearsal. The authorities took their seats and the play began.[2] At once he cried out that this was no work of an author but of a thief who should not get away with it – that there was already a *Flatterer* in existence, an old play of Naevius and Plautus, from which the characters of the sponger and the soldier had been taken.

If that is a fault, it is due to inadvertence, not to any intention on the author's part to plagiarize. You, the audience,

1. Luscius Lanuvinus, Terence's rival and critic.
2. The only reference we have to this sort of censorship of plays.

will soon be able to judge if this is so. Certainly Menander's *Flatterer* exists, and in it there are a sponger who flatters and a soldier who boasts. The author admits that he has transferred these characters from the Greek play into his *Eunuch*: but the suggestion that he knew that these plays had already been translated into Latin he absolutely denies. If he is not allowed to make use of the same characters as other writers, how can he still bring on a running slave, virtuous wives and dishonest courtesans, greedy spongers and braggart soldiers? How can he show substitution of a child, deception of an old man by his slave, love, hatred, and suspicion? Nothing in fact is ever said which has not been said before.

It is only right that you should recognize this, and forgive new authors if they do what earlier writers have often done. Give us your support, pay attention in silence, and hear what *The Eunuch* has to say.

CHARACTERS

LACHES	an Athenian gentleman
PHAEDRIA	his elder son, in love with Thais
CHAEREA	his younger son, in love with Pamphila
ANTIPHO	a friend of Chaerea's
CHREMES	a young countryman of Attica
THRASO	an army officer
GNATHO	his hanger-on
DORUS	a eunuch
PARMENO	Laches' chief slave, attendant on Phaedria
DONAX	
SANGA	
SIMALIO	slaves of Thraso
SYRISCUS	
Two others	
THAIS	a courtesan
PYTHIAS	her maidservant and chief slave
DORIAS	slaves of Thais
Two other maids	
PAMPHILA	Chremes' young sister, at present a slave of Thraso's
SOPHRONA	her old nurse
An Ethiopian girl slave	

*

The scene is laid in Athens in front of the houses of Laches
and Thais. To the audience's right the street leads to the
centre of the town and the harbour and docks of the Peiraeus,
and to their left to the countryside of Attica

[*The young man* PHAEDRIA *comes out of his father's house talking to his slave* PARMENO, *a middle-aged attendant.*]

PHAEDRIA: Well then, what am I to do? I can't refuse to go now she's asking me herself, can I? Or had I better think of making a stand against these insults from such women? She slammed her door on me once, and now she opens it again, but shall I go back? No, not if she goes down on bended knees.

PARMENO: Of course, Sir, if you can do that, it's the best and boldest course. But if you make a start and can't stick it out, and then go running back to her when you can't stand it any longer, unasked and no terms fixed, letting her see you're in love and can't bear it – then it'll all be over and done with. It will be the end of *you*, Sir; she'll stop play once she finds you're beaten. So while there's time, do think, and think hard, Sir. Reason can't solve what hasn't got rhyme nor reason, and all these upsets – insults, jealousies, quarrels, reconciliations, war, then peace again – they're all part of love, and if you insist on a method to settle all your uncertainties, why, you might as well think up a method for madness. You're angry now, muttering away to yourself: 'I'll show her! She ... with him ... and me ... and then not ... just let her try! I'd rather die! She'll learn what sort of a man I am!' But believe me, it won't take more than a single tiny false tear – which she can hardly squeeze out by force after all that rubbing of her eyes – to damp down all those hot words. Then she'll turn the attack on you, and you'll be the one to suffer.

PHAEDRIA: Monstrous! At last I can see her wickedness and my own sorry state. I'm eaten up with love and I'm sick of

it, I'm dying on my feet, eyes open, awake and aware, but
what on earth can I do?

PARMENO: Do? Buy your freedom as cheap as possible, and
if you can't get it cheap, pay up what you can and stop
worrying yourself to death.

PHAEDRIA: That's your advice?

PARMENO: Yes, if you've any sense. Love provides enough
troubles anyway – just you face up to those properly and
don't go adding to them. Look, she's coming out, that
blight on our fortunes! Every penny we ought to have goes
to *her*.

[THAIS *comes out of her house without seeing them: she is an*
attractive young woman.]

THAIS: Oh dear, I'm afraid Phaedria was annoyed and misunderstood me when I wouldn't let him in yesterday.

PHAEDRIA [*clutching* PARMENO]: The mere sight of her sets
me trembling and shivering.

PARMENO: Courage, Sir! Go nearer the fire and you'll warm
up all right.

THAIS [*coming forward*]: Who's that? Phaedria my dear, is that
you? Why are you waiting here? You should have come
straight in.

PARMENO: Not a word about shutting her door to him!

THAIS: Why don't you say something?

PHAEDRIA [*bitterly*]: I always find the door open, don't I –
always come first with you.

THAIS: Please, no more.

PHAEDRIA: Why 'no more'? Oh Thaïs, Thaïs, if only love
meant the same thing to you as it does to me! I wish you
suffered for this as much as I do, or I could think nothing
of what you have done!

THAIS: Phaedria, my own, my darling, don't torture yourself, please. I swear I didn't do this because I care for anyone

or love anyone more than you. It was a thing which had to be done.

PARMENO: Quite so. Poor soul, I suppose you shut the door for love of him!

THAIS: You think that of me, Parmeno? All right: but let me tell you why I sent for you.

PHAEDRIA [*eagerly*]: Tell me.

THAIS: First of all, can *he* keep his mouth shut?

PARMENO: Me? Of course I can. I stick to a promise – but there are conditions. When I hear the truth spoken I can hold my tongue and keep quiet as well as anyone, but if it's a lie or an invention or a trumped-up tale, it's out at once; I'm full of cracks and leak all over. So if you want a secret kept, Madam, tell the truth.

THAIS [*ignoring him*]: My mother came from Samos and lived in Rhodes.

PARMENO: I can keep *that* secret.

THAIS: While she was there, a merchant made her a present of a little girl stolen from here, from Attica.

PHAEDRIA: Athenian born?

THAIS: I think so, but we can't be sure. All she could tell us herself was her father's and mother's name, and she didn't know her country or anything else to identify her – she was too young. The merchant added that he had heard from the pirates who sold her that she had been carried off from Sunium. As soon as my mother had taken her in she took care to teach her all she could and bring her up as her own child. She was generally believed to be my sister. Then I found a protector, my first and only one, and came here to Athens with him. It was he who set me up with all I have.

PARMENO: Two lies: they'll both leak out.

THAIS: What do you mean?

PARMENO: One wasn't enough for you and he wasn't the

only one to give you something. My master here has also
made a handsome contribution.

THAIS: Very well, but let me come to my point. It wasn'
long before my soldier friend went off to Caria, and tha
was when I came to know you. You know yourself how
dear you have been to me ever since and how I have alway:
told you everything.

PHAEDRIA [*bitterly*]: There's another thing for Parmeno tc
let out.

PARMENO: No doubt about that, Sir.

THAIS: Please listen, both of you. My mother died recently
at Rhodes, leaving a brother who is always greedy fo
money. Seeing the girl was a beauty and could sing to th
lyre, he hoped she would fetch a good price, so he put he
up for sale and sold her on the spot. Luckily my frienc
happened to be there and bought her as a present for me
knowing nothing of course of all I've just told you. Now
he's back in Athens, but since he found out about my relations with you he's busy finding excuses not to give m
her. He says he'd be willing to do so if he could be sure h
came first with me and wasn't afraid I should leave him
once I had her, only that is what he *is* afraid of. But I have
my suspicions that he's taken a fancy to the girl.

PHAEDRIA: Is it more than a fancy?

THAIS: No; I have made inquiries. Now there are many
reasons, Phaedria dear, why I want to get her away from
him. In the first place she's spoken of as my sister, and then
there's the chance I may be able to restore her to her
family. I'm alone here, Phaedria, without a single friend or
relative, and I should like to make some friends by doing a
kindness. Please help me with this and make things easier:
let the man have first place with me for the next few days.
. . . Can't you answer me?

PHAEDRIA: You wretched woman, what answer can I give to conduct like yours?

PARMENO: Well done, Sir, congratulations! It's come home to you at last; you're a man!

PHAEDRIA: Do you think I couldn't see what you were leading up to? 'A little girl was carried off from here, my mother brought her up as her own, she was taken for my sister and I want to get her away to restore her to her family.' In fact all you've just said amounts to this – I'm kept out and he's let in. And why? Obviously because you love him more than you love me; and now you're afraid that girl he brought here may snatch him from you – for what he's worth.

THAIS: *I'm* afraid of *that*?

PHAEDRIA: What else is worrying you? Tell me that. Is he the only one who gives you presents? Have you ever known me set a limit to my generosity? When you told me you wanted a black slave-girl, didn't I leave everything to look for one? And then you said you'd like a eunuch because only queens employ them; well, I've found one, and only yesterday I paid two thousand drachmas for the pair. Badly treated as I was by you, I didn't forget; and in return for what I've done you kick me out!

THAIS: There, there, Phaedria. I want to get the girl away and I still think my plan is the best way to do this, but rather than lose your affection I'll do anything you bid me.

PHAEDRIA: If only you spoke from your heart and really meant 'rather than lose your affection'! If only I could believe you are sincere in what you say, I could endure anything!

PARMENO [*aside*]: He's weakening. Beaten by a word and all too soon!

THAIS: Alas, don't I speak from the heart? Have you ever

wanted anything from me, even in fun, without getting it? *I* can ask, but I can't persuade you to give me a mere couple of days.

PHAEDRIA: If it's only a couple . . . but it might turn into twenty.

THAIS: I promise you, only a couple or –

PHAEDRIA: I'm not having 'or'.

THAIS: It shan't be more. Just let me have this.

PHAEDRIA: Oh all right, have it your own way.

THAIS [*embracing him*]: No wonder I love you, you're so kind.

PHAEDRIA: I'll leave town and endure my misery in the country – two days of it. That's settled then; Thais must have her way. Parmeno, see that those two are brought across.

PARMENO: Very good, Sir.

PHAEDRIA: For two days then, Thais – good-bye.

THAIS: Good-bye, dear Phaedria. That's all, then?

PHAEDRIA: All – except this. When you are with your soldier in person, be absent in spirit. Night and day, love me, long for me, dream of me, wait for me, think of me, hope for me, find joy in me, and be all mine. You have my heart: try to give me yours.

   [*He walks firmly into* LACHES' *house without a backward glance, followed by* PARMENO.]

THAIS: Oh dear. . . . Perhaps he doesn't trust me and judges my character by other women. . . . But knowing myself, I can swear I've told nothing but the truth, and no man is dearer to me than my Phaedria. All I have done I did for the girl's sake, for I have hopes that I've already found her brother, a young man of good family. He's arranged to visit me this very day, so I'll go in and wait for him.

   [*She goes into her house. After a short pause* PHAEDRIA *comes out, ready for departure, followed by* PARMENO.]

PHAEDRIA: Do as I told you and have those two brought here.

PARMENO: Yes, Sir.

PHAEDRIA: Get on with it!

PARMENO: Yes, Sir.

PHAEDRIA: Look sharp!

PARMENO: Yes, Sir.

PHAEDRIA: You know your instructions?

PARMENO: What a question! There's no difficulty about it. I only wish, Sir, you were likely to get as much out of this as you're going to lose by it.

PHAEDRIA: I'm lost anyway, that's the worst thing. . . . But don't *you* go making heavy weather of it.

PARMENO: I won't. I'll see it's done. Anything else?

PHAEDRIA: Say the best you can about my present, and do what you can to keep that rival of mine away from her.

PARMENO: No need to remind me about *that*.

PHAEDRIA: Now I'm off to the country and there I'll stay.

PARMENO: That's right, Sir.

PHAEDRIA: Just a minute –

PARMENO: What is it?

PHAEDRIA: Do you think I shall be able to stick it out and not come home too soon?

PARMENO: Good lord, no, Sir. You'll be back at once, or at any rate after the first sleepless night.

PHAEDRIA: I shall make sure I'm so tired I'll sleep in spite of myself.

PARMENO: Then all you'll gain is that you'll be sleepless *and* tired.

PHAEDRIA: Shut up, Parmeno, that's nonsense. I'm absolutely determined from now on to be *firm*. I've been letting myself go. . . . Why, if it came to it, I could do without her for – *three* whole days.

PARMENO: Three days on end? Be careful what you say, Sir.

PHAEDRIA: I've made up my mind.

[*He goes off left with a great air of determination.*]

PARMENO: Oh love! What a damn queer disease it is that
changes a man so much you'd hardly know him for the
same! There was a time when no one was as sensible,
serious, and sober as this young man. . . . But who's that
coming? Why, it's Gnatho, that hanger-on of the soldier's,
and he's got the girl with him to give to Thais. God, what a
beauty! I'll cut a poor figure today with my decrepit old
eunuch. This girl's even better looking than Thais herself.

[*He stands back as* GNATHO *comes on from the right, followed
by* PAMPHILA *and a maid, and voices his self-satisfaction to
the audience.*]

GNATHO: Ye gods, how one man can surpass another! What
a world of difference there is between a fool and a man
with brains! The thought struck me on my way here, when
I ran into a man of my own rank and position, a decent
fellow who'd guzzled up all his patrimony like I did. There
he was, unshaven, dirty, and wretched, a ragged old man.
'What's the meaning of this get-up?' I said. 'I've been unfortunate, lost all I had, and look what I've come to. All my
friends and acquaintances cut me now.' He filled me with
contempt when I compared him with myself. 'You great
booby,' I said, 'have you managed to lose all your self-
confidence? Did your wits disappear along with your fortune? Look at me; my origins are the same as yours; I'm
healthy, well-groomed, and properly dressed, a fine figure
of a man. I'm penniless, but I've got everything: I've
nothing of my own and lack nothing.' 'But unfortunately I
haven't the talent for playing the fool or taking a beating.'
'Are you supposing that's how it's done? You're quite
wrong. There was a time, a generation ago, when there
was money to be made by that kind of thing, but we've new

ways of setting our traps today. I can even claim to be the
inventor of the new method. There's a type of man, you
know, who wants to come first in everything and doesn't
quite make it. They're the ones I aim at, but I don't try to
make them laugh at me – no, no, I'm ready with *my* laughs
and admiration for them and their wit. I praise whatever
they say, and then if they change to the opposite I praise
that too. If they say No, I say No, and if it's Yes, it's Yes
from me too. In fact, I've trained myself to agree with
anything. There's a fat lot to be made out of it today, I
can tell you.'

PARMENO [*aside*]: That's a clever one! He can turn a fool
into a gibbering idiot in no time.

GNATHO [*still not seeing him*]: During this conversation we
came to the market, and up came running the confec-
tioners, fishmongers, butchers, cooks, poulterers, and sprat-
sellers, all delighted to see me, people who'd profited from
me when I still had money and still often do now I've none.
They always greet me, ask me to dinner, and bid me welcome. When that poor starveling saw the honours paid me
and my easy way of making a living, he began to beg me to
let him learn from me. I told him he could be my follower;
the philosophers have schools named after them, so I have
hopes that spongers may henceforth be known as Gna-
thonists.

PARMENO [*aside*]: Look what can be got out of idleness and
eating with someone else to foot the bill!

GNATHO: But I must hurry on to give this girl to Thais and
ask her to dine with my master. Why, there's Parmeno
standing outside the house. He's our rival's servant, and
he looks pretty glum, so all must be going well. They
must be having a cool reception. I can't resist teasing the
fellow.

PARMENO [*aside*]: And men like this imagine that it only
 takes a present to make Thais theirs!

GNATHO [*going up to him ceremoniously*]: Gnatho bids a warm
 welcome to his dear friend Parmeno. How do I find you?

PARMENO: Standing on my feet.

GNATHO: So I see. Is there anything here [*eyeing the girl*] you
 would prefer not to see?

PARMENO: You.

GNATHO: Quite so, but is there anything else?

PARMENO: Why should there be?

GNATHO: You look glum.

PARMENO: It's nothing.

GNATHO: Well then, cheer up. What do you think of this for
 a slave girl?

PARMENO: Not bad.

GNATHO [*aside*]: He's warming up.

PARMENO [*overhearing*]: That's just where he's wrong.

GNATHO: How do you think Thais will like this present?

PARMENO: Do you mean by this that we're turned out?
 Well, it's a world of ups and downs.

GNATHO: Mark my words, Parmeno, I'm giving you six
 whole months of peace from running to and fro and staying
 up till daybreak. Isn't that something to look forward to?

PARMENO: Very kind of you, I'm sure.

GNATHO: I always try to please my friends.

PARMENO: Congratulations.

GNATHO: Don't let me keep you if you were on your way
 somewhere.

PARMENO: I wasn't.

GNATHO [*eagerly*]: In that case, please do me a small favour;
 help me to gain admission to Thais.

PARMENO: You've only got to go in; now you've that girl
 with you the doors will open of their own accord.

[GNATHO *tries the door and it opens.*]

GNATHO: Perhaps there's someone I can send out to you?

[*He goes in with* PAMPHILA *and the maid.*]

PARMENO [*shouting after him*]: Just you wait till those two
   days are up! You can open doors with your little finger
   now your luck's in, but I'll see you're kept kicking at them
   without an answer!

GNATHO [*coming out*]: Still there, Parmeno? I wonder if you
   were left to intercept any private message passing between
   my master and the lady?

PARMENO: Witty, aren't you, just the type to please your
   soldier friend. [GNATHO *goes off right.*] Now I do believe I
   see my master's younger son coming. He's supposed to be
   on guard duty at the docks today, so I wonder what brings
   him here. Something's up – he's in such a hurry and search-
   ing everywhere.

[CHAEREA *rushes on from the right, not seeing* PARMENO:
   he is a very young man in officer's uniform.]

CHAEREA: Hell! The girl's lost and I'm lost too in losing
   sight of her. Where to look, where to find her, whom to
   ask, or which way to turn I've no idea. My only hope is
   that her whereabouts can't stay hidden for long. Oh she's
   a beauty! I've written off all other women – I'm through
   with ordinary types.

PARMENO [*aside*]: Now here's the other one talking about
   love! Oh my poor old master! If once this boy begins
   there's no knowing where the fit will take him; you'll say
   the first one was just fooling about.

CHAEREA: Devil take the old fool who kept me, and me too
   for stopping and paying attention to him. But look who's
   there – hullo, Parmeno.

PARMENO: What's the matter with you? what's all the fuss
   about? Where've you come from?

CHAEREA: Damned if I know – either where I've come from or where I'm going.   I've completely lost my head.

PARMENO: How on earth?

CHAEREA [*impressively*]: I'm in love.

PARMENO: What?

CHAEREA: Now's your chance, Parmeno, to show what sort of a man you are. You know the promise you often made me: 'Just you find something to love, Sir, and I'll show you how useful I can be.' That was when I used to bring all the contents of my father's larder secretly to your room.

PARMENO: Don't be so silly.

CHAEREA: Well, now I've done it; I've found someone to love. Now you can please keep your promise – if it's a case you think is worth your while. This isn't an ordinary girl, like the ones whose mothers want them to have round shoulders and flat chests to make them look slim – and if there's one who's a bit more attractive they tell her she looks like a prize-fighter and cut down her diet, so that she ends up after treatment thin as a bulrush in spite of her natural charms.

PARMENO: What about your girl?

CHAEREA: *She*'s something quite remarkable.

PARMENO: She would be!

CHAEREA: Natural complexion, firm figure, plump and juicy . . .

PARMENO: Age?

CHAEREA: Sixteen.

PARMENO: A perfect peach!

CHAEREA: You must get her for me, Parmeno, by force or stealth – or prayer; I don't care how, so long as I have her.

PARMENO: Well, who does she belong to?

CHAEREA: I've no idea.

PARMENO: Where does she come from?

CHAEREA: Don't know.

PARMENO: Where does she live?

CHAEREA: Don't know that either.

PARMENO: Where did you see her?

CHAEREA: In the street.

PARMENO: How did you come to lose her?

CHAEREA: That was what I was cursing myself for as I came along. I don't think there's another man alive whose good luck turns against him like mine. Oh, what a dirty trick! I can't bear it.

PARMENO: But what *happened*?

CHAEREA: I'll tell you. You know Archimedes, that old friend of my father's –

PARMENO: Yes, of course.

CHAEREA: I ran into him while I was following the girl.

PARMENO: How inconvenient.

CHAEREA: Inconvenient's not strong enough – I'd call it damned unlucky. I can swear I haven't set eyes on the man for the last six or seven months and I had to meet him now when I least wanted or needed him. A bird of ill omen, that's what I'd call him – wouldn't you?

PARMENO: I would indeed.

CHAEREA: He came running up from a mile off, hunched-up and shaking, with his slobbering old mouth wheezing away: 'Hi, Chaerea, I'm calling you!' he said. I stopped. 'Do you know what I want you for?' 'No, tell me.' 'I've got a case on tomorrow.' 'So what?' 'Be sure to tell your father not to forget to come early to support me.' It took him an hour to get this out, and then I asked if I could go. 'Certainly,' he said, and I made off, but when I looked round for the girl she'd just turned off this way, down our street.

PARMENO [*aside*]: I do believe he means the girl who's just
been given to Thais.

CHAEREA: By the time I was here she'd disappeared.

PARMENO: I suppose she'd someone with her?

CHAEREA: Yes, one of those spongers and a maid.

PARMENO [*aside*]: It's her all right. [*To* CHAEREA] Come off
it, Sir; the affair's finished, dead and buried.

CHAEREA: I don't know what you're talking about.

PARMENO: I mean *your* affair.

CHAEREA: But do you know who she is? Have you seen her?

PARMENO: I've seen her, I know her, and I can tell you where
she was taken.

CHAEREA [*shaking him excitedly*]: Parmeno, old man, do you
really know her? And where she is now?

PARMENO: She was brought here as a present for Thais and
given to her.

CHAEREA: Who's able to make a present like that?

PARMENO: The soldier Thraso, Phaedria's rival.

CHAEREA: That doesn't leave my brother much of a part.

PARMENO: No, and you'd say so even more if you knew
the present he's intending to give her himself.

CHAEREA: Well, what is it?

PARMENO: A eunuch.

CHAEREA: No, please, not that horrible individual, that old
woman of a man you bought yesterday!

PARMENO: That's the one.

CHAEREA: He'll be kicked out and his present after him. But
I didn't know Thais lived near us.

PARMENO: She hasn't for long.

CHAEREA: Damn it all, I've never even seen her! Come on,
Parmeno, is she as lovely as they say?

PARMENO: She is.

CHAEREA: But doesn't bear comparison with my girl?

PARMENO: Ah no, that's different.

CHAEREA: Parmeno, for God's sake help me to possess her!

PARMENO: I'll do my best, I'll try everything I can. Now, Sir, may I go?

CHAEREA: Where to?

PARMENO: Home. I've got to fetch those slaves your brother told me to give to Thais.

CHAEREA: Oh, lucky eunuch, to be a present for that house!

PARMENO: What do you mean?

CHAEREA: Can't you see? He'll always see his fellow slave in all her beauty around the house, he'll speak to her and be under the same roof, he may sometimes take his meals with her . . . and perhaps sleep by her side.

PARMENO [teasing him]: Suppose you were the lucky one –

CHAEREA: How could I be?

PARMENO: You could wear his clothes –

CHAEREA: His clothes? And then?

PARMENO: I could take you in instead of him –

CHAEREA: Yes –

PARMENO: And say you were him –

CHAEREA: I see!

PARMENO: You could enjoy all those advantages you just said would be his; be near her, eat with her, touch her, play with her – and sleep by her side. None of the women there can recognize you or knows who you are. [Bursts out laughing] Besides, you're just the right age and figure to be taken for a eunuch!

CHAEREA [ignoring this]: Splendid! I've never had such marvellous advice. Quick, come home at once, dress me up, bring me out, take me there this minute!

PARMENO: What? Oh no, I was only pulling your leg.

CHAEREA: Nonsense!

PARMENO: I'm a damn fool – what have I done? Where are you shoving me? You'll have me down. Stop it, I say!

CHAEREA: Come *on*.

PARMENO: You're really set on it?

CHAEREA: Of course I am.

PARMENO: You'll find things too hot for you if you don't look out.

CHAEREA: No I shan't. Let me do it.

PARMENO: Yes, but it'll be me who pays for it.

CHAEREA [*impatiently*]: Oh –

PARMENO: We'll be doing wrong.

CHAEREA: *Wrong?* For me to be taken into a house of that reputation and pay back those tormentors who always scorn us and our youth and think up every kind of torture for us? Wrong for me to pay them back and deceive them as they do us? Would you rather I duped my father? I'd be blamed all right for that if I was found out, but everyone will think this a deed well done.

PARMENO: All right, if you must do it, go ahead. Only don't go putting the blame on me later on.

CHAEREA: Of course not.

PARMENO: I'm to take it as an order then?

CHAEREA [*drawing himself up*]: Order? It's my will and command. I'm not one to shirk responsibility. Follow me.

PARMENO: And heaven be on our side!

[*They go into* LACHES' *house. Soon* GNATHO *and his master* THRASO, *a middle-aged army officer, come on from the right.*]

THRASO: Thais really sent me many thanks?

GNATHO: Her heartfelt thanks.

THRASO: And she's really pleased?

GNATHO: Not so much pleased with the gift as with the fact that you were the giver. That's a real triumph for her.

PARMENO [*opening* LACHES' *door*]: I must watch for the right moment to take him across. Oh, there's the soldier.

THRASO [*complacently*]: I have a real knack of doing what will please.

GNATHO: That is something which has always struck me.

THRASO: The king always thanked me most warmly in his own person for anything I did, in a way he never thanked anyone else.

GNATHO: It often happens that others work hard to win the praise which a word from a shrewd man like yourself can make his own.

THRASO: True.

GNATHO: Thus the king held you –

THRASO: He did indeed –

GNATHO: – in high favour.

THRASO: Yes; he entrusted his entire army to me, and all his plans.

GNATHO: How wonderful!

THRASO: Then when he was bored with his courtiers or tired of business and felt he needed a rest, as if – do you know?

GNATHO: I do: as if he would rid his mind of all his troubles –

THRASO: You've got it. At such times he would take me aside as his sole companion.

GNATHO: Ah, there's a king with good taste!

THRASO: That's the man he is; very select in his company.

GNATHO [*aside*]: *Very* select, if he chose you.

THRASO: All the court was jealous, backbiters all, but what did I care? They were miserably envious, most of all the man in charge of the Indian elephants. When he was particularly troublesome, 'Why, Strato,' I used to say, 'have you learnt ferocity from those wild beasts of yours?'

GNATHO: A pretty bit of wit! You had him there. What did he do?

THRASO: Struck dumb.

GNATHO: I'm not surprised.

PARMENO [*aside*]: Good lord, what a hopeless fool the man is! And the other's a wicked liar.

THRASO: Did I ever tell you, Gnatho, about the dinner-party where I dealt with that man from Rhodes?

GNATHO: Never; do tell me now. [*Aside*] I've heard it thousands of times.

THRASO: This young fellow from Rhodes I was talking about was dining with me. I had a girl there, and he was cracking jokes at my expense. 'Less of your impudence,' I said: 'Why should you be a hare who runs with the hounds?'

[GNATHO *breaks into exaggerated laughter at this pointless platitude.*]

THRASO: What did you say?

GNATHO: Brilliant! Witty! Neat! The best thing I've heard. Is it yours? I thought it was an old one.

THRASO: Had you heard it before?

GNATHO: Often, and it always goes down well.

THRASO: It's my own.

GNATHO: He must have felt it, the forward young idiot.

PARMENO [*aside*]: To hell with you!

GNATHO: What did he say?

THRASO: It finished him. Everyone present nearly died of laughter. Since then they've all stood in awe of me.

GNATHO: And so they should.

THRASO: By the way, what about this girl: should I rid Thais of her suspicions that I'm attracted to her?

GNATHO: Certainly not. You'd do better to increase them.

THRASO: Why?

GNATHO: Why? You know how it galls you if ever she praises Phaedria or even mentions his name?

THRASO: Yes, yes, I know.

GNATHO: There's only one way of stopping it. When she names Phaedria, you retaliate with Pamphila; if ever she suggests asking Phaedria in to supper, we'll invite Pamphila to sing, and if she praises his good looks, you praise hers. We can give her tit for tat and cut her to the quick.

THRASO [*sighing*]: If only she really loved me, Gnatho, that would be the thing to do.

GNATHO: She waits in for your presents and loves *them*, so I believe she's loved you for a long time; and it's long been easy for you to hurt her, since she's always afraid of losing what she gets out of you now if you go off in a huff elsewhere.

THRASO: True: I hadn't thought of that.

GNATHO: You're joking – it's just that you hadn't given your mind to it. Otherwise you'd have thought of it yourself, and how much better!

[THAIS *comes out of her house.*]

THAIS: I'm sure I heard my soldier's voice – and there he is. Welcome, Thraso.

THRASO: Thais, my own, my sweetheart, how are you? Can you love your Thraso a little bit for the girl he's given you?

PARMENO [*aside*]: There's gallantry! What a way to start!

THAIS: Very much, as you deserve.

THRASO: Then come along to dinner; why delay?

PARMENO [*aside*]: Listen to him now! The man's sub-human.

THAIS: When you like; I won't keep you waiting.

PARMENO [*aside*]: Here's my cue – I can pretend I've just come out. [*Comes forward*] Are you going out, Madam?

THAIS: Ah, Parmeno, I'm obliged to you. I'm just going –

PARMENO: Where?

THAIS: Can't you see? [*indicating* THRASO].

PARMENO: Oh I'm sick of seeing *him*. When it suits you, Madam, I've presents for you from Phaedria.

THRASO: Must we stand around? Why can't we go?

PARMENO: By your leave, Sir, I'm only asking for a moment to give the lady what we have for her and just say a few words.

THRASO: Fine presents, comparable no doubt with my own!

PARMENO: We shall see. [*Calls inside the house*] Here, hurry along with those two I told to come out. [*The black slave-girl comes out.*] Come forward, you. [*To* THAIS] Now *she's* come all the way from Ethiopia.

THRASO: Three hundred drachmas at the most!

GNATHO: Scarcely that.

PARMENO: Where are you, Dorus? [CHAEREA *comes out, dressed suitably for a eunuch.*] Now there's a eunuch for you, in the prime of life and looks like a gentleman!

THRASO [*clearly interested*]: Heavens, he is good looking.

PARMENO: Well, Gnatho? Any criticisms? What about you, Sir? Silence speaks volumes. Test him on literature, music, athletics: I'll guarantee his accomplishments come up to any young gentleman's.

THRASO: I know what I'd do to that eunuch if it came to it – drunk or sober.

PARMENO [*to* THAIS]: And the donor of these gifts is not making demands on you to live with him alone, to the exclusion of everyone else. *He* doesn't recount his battles and display his scars or lie in wait for you like someone else I know. All he asks is to be received when it's convenient and you have time and feel like it.

THRASO: The man's master must be a penniless and poor-spirited creature!

GNATHO: Obviously no one with means to buy another would put up with a slave like this!

PARMENO: You shut up, you scum of the earth. I know you and your nasty ways, making up to *his* type. You'd steal from a corpse.

THRASO: Are – we – going?

THAIS: I must just take these two indoors and give some instructions. I shan't be a minute. [*She goes in with the black slave and* CHAEREA.]

THRASO [*to* GNATHO]: I shall go. You wait here for her.

PARMENO: The High Command shouldn't be seen in the street with its lady friend!

THRASO: All I wish to say to *you* is – you take after your master.

[PARMENO *goes off laughing, down the street, right, while* GNATHO *tries to conceal his laughter.*]

THRASO [*suspiciously*]: What are you laughing at?

GNATHO: Only something you said just now – and that tale about the man from Rhodes, whenever I think of it. But here comes Thais.

[THAIS *comes out with her maids,* PYTHIAS, *a middle-aged woman, and two others.*]

THRASO: You hurry on ahead then, and have everything ready at home.

GNATHO: I will. [*He goes off right.*]

THAIS: Look after them well, Pythias, and if Chremes should call, try first to persuade him to wait; if it doesn't suit him ask him to call again, and if he can't manage that, bring him to me.

PYTHIAS: Very good, Madam.

THAIS: Now, was there anything else? Yes, take great care of the girl, and all of you stay indoors.

THRASO: Can't we *go*?

THAIS [*to the two maids*]: You follow me.

> [PYTHIAS *goes back into the house;* THRASO *and* THAIS *go off right. After a short pause,* CHREMES *comes on from the left. A shy and awkward young man, he pauses doubtfully outside* THAIS' *door and then turns away.*]

CHREMES: The more I think of it, the more I'm convinced Thais has something unpleasant in store for me, she's been working on me so artfully from the moment she first asked me to visit her. [*To audience*] (In case any of you are wondering about my relations with her, I may say I didn't even know the woman.) When I called she found an excuse for keeping me waiting – said she'd been at her prayers and had something important to discuss with me. From then on I had suspicions this was all a plot. She sat down beside me in a familiar way and tried to start a conversation. When it petered out, she changed the subject. How long had my parents been dead? A long time, I said. Then she asked if I had any property at Sunium and how far it was from the sea. I suppose she's taken a fancy to it and hopes to get it from me. Lastly, had I had a little sister who disappeared from there, was anyone with her, had she anything on her and could anyone identify her? Why on earth does she want to know all this? Surely she can't have the nerve to pretend *she* is the little sister who was lost years ago – if the girl's still alive she'd be no more than sixteen, and Thais is older than I am. Now she's sent for me again, begging me to come. Either she must say what she wants or stop making a nuisance of herself. I'm damned if I'll come a third time. [*Knocks on the door*] Hi there, is anyone at home? It's Chremes.

PYTHIAS [*comes out and greets him eagerly*]: Oh, my dear young Sir, how good of you to come!

CHREMES [*aside*]: I said there was a plot.

PYTHIAS: My mistress left an urgent message for you, asking you to call again tomorrow.

CHREMES: I shan't be in town.

PYTHIAS: Please, Sir –

CHREMES: Impossible, I tell you.

PYTHIAS: Then will you please wait here till she returns?

CHREMES: Certainly not.

PYTHIAS: My dear Sir, why not?

CHREMES: Go to the devil!

PYTHIAS: If you are sure you can't stay, will you please step across to where she is?

CHREMES [*sulkily*]: Very well.

PYTHIAS [*calling indoors*]: Dorias! Take this gentleman over to Thraso's at once.

[*A maid comes out of the house and goes off right with* CHREMES. *Soon after,* ANTIPHO *hurries on from the right, a cheerful young man also in uniform.*]

ANTIPHO: Some of the lads at the docks met yesterday and planned to club together for dinner today. We chose Chaerea to make the arrangements, fixed the time and place, and pledged ourselves to be there. The time's passed, nothing's ready in the place we named, and Chaerea's nowhere to be found. Now the others have given me the job of looking for him and I've come to see if he's at home. [THAIS' *door opens and* CHAEREA *appears.*] There's someone coming out – is it him or isn't it? It is – but what on earth's happened to the man? Dressed up like that – what's he up to? It beats me. . . . I can't imagine. . . . Whatever it is, I think I'll just step back for the moment and see if I can find out.

CHAEREA [*in a state of wild elation*]: Anyone here? Nobody. Anyone follow me from home? Not a soul. Dare I be happy and let myself go? My God, this is the moment to

face death while I can bear it, before life's troubles spoil my
happiness! And there's no busybody wanting to follow
wherever I lead, deafening me with questions and pestering
me to death to know why I'm so excited and happy, where
I'm going, where I've come from, where I got these clothes
and what I want with them, whether I'm off my head or
not!

ANTIPHO: I'll go and do him the service he seems to want.
Chaerea, why are you so excited? What's the meaning of
these clothes? Why are you so happy? What's the idea?
Are you off your head? Why are you staring at me – can't
you answer?

CHAEREA [*hugging him wildly*]: Oh glorious day! Oh my dear
friend, welcome! The very man I wanted to see!

ANTIPHO: For heaven's sake tell me what's up.

CHAEREA: Then please listen while I tell you. You know that
girl of my brother's?

ANTIPHO: Yes of course; I suppose you mean Thais.

CHAEREA: That's the one.

ANTIPHO: I thought so.

CHAEREA: Today she's been given a girl . . . no need for me to
say much in praise of *her* looks. You know I've a con-
noisseur's eye for a lovely woman. I fell for this one.

ANTIPHO: Really?

CHAEREA: You'd give her top marks if you saw her. To cut it
short, I'm in love. By a stroke of luck there was a eunuch
at home that my brother had bought for Thais and not yet
sent to her. Our man Parmeno made a suggestion which I
jumped at –

ANTIPHO: What was it?

CHAEREA: Shut up and you'll hear. To change clothes with
him and have myself taken there in his place.

ANTIPHO: Instead of the eunuch?

CHAEREA: Yes.

ANTIPHO: What on earth were you to gain by that?

CHAEREA: Why, it's obvious. I could see and hear her and be with the object of my desires. Wasn't that a good scheme? Not a bad bit of planning, Antipho. I was handed over to the lady, she accepted me and was delighted to take me into her house. She put the girl in my care.

ANTIPHO: *Your* care?

CHAEREA: Mine.

ANTIPHO: Care and protection, I suppose. . . .

CHAEREA: She gave instructions that no man was to come near the girl and told me not to go out but to stay alone with her safely inside the house. I bowed modestly, eyes on the ground. [*He does so.*]

ANTIPHO: Silly fool!

CHAEREA: 'I am going out to dinner,' said Thais, and off she went with her maids, leaving a few new young ones to wait on the girl. They began at once to get her ready for a bath, while I kept telling them to hurry. Meanwhile the girl sat in her room, looking up at a picture on the wall which showed the story of Jupiter pouring the shower of gold into Danaë's lap.[1] I began to look at it too, and my spirits soared to think how he had played the same game long ago; a god turning himself into a man and crawling secretly across another man's roof, coming down to seduce a woman – down through the skylight! And what a god! 'who shakes the topmost towers of heaven with his thunder.'[2] Couldn't a mere man like me do the same? He could – and gladly. During these meditations of mine, the girl was summoned to her bath. She went, had it, and came back. Then the maids settled her on a couch. I stood around

1. See St Augustine, *Confessions*, ch. 16.

2. According to Donatus, a parody of the poet Ennius.

to see if they had any orders for me. Then one came up and said: 'Here, Dorus, take this fan, fan her gently with it while we have a bath, and when we've finished you can have one too if you like.' I took it with a bad grace.

ANTIPHO: What wouldn't I give to have seen your shameless face and the figure you cut, you great ass, standing there with a fan in your hand!

CHAEREA: The words were hardly out of her mouth when there was a rush for the door. They all went off to the bath, chattering as servants do when they're alone in the house. The girl meanwhile fell asleep. I took a secret peep at her, sideways behind the fan, like this, and at the same time looked round to make sure the coast was clear. It was. Then I bolted the door.

ANTIPHO: What then?

CHAEREA: What do you mean, 'what then', you fool?

ANTIPHO: Oh, all right.

CHAEREA: Was I to lose the chance offered me, such an opportunity so brief, so unhoped for and so much desired? My God, if I had, I should really have been what I pretended.

ANTIPHO: True, as you say. Incidentally, what have you done about our dinner?

CHAEREA: It's ready.

ANTIPHO: Good man! Where? At your house?

CHAEREA: No, no, at Discus'.

ANTIPHO: What a way! All the more reason for us to hurry. Change your clothes.

CHAEREA: Where on earth can I change? I must keep away from home in case my brother's there; or my father might have got back from the country by now.

ANTIPHO: Let's go to my place, it's the nearest, and you can change there.

CHAEREA: Good, come on. On the way we can be planning
　how I can really make this girl my own.

ANTIPHO: Right you are.

　　[*They go off right together, and after a pause the maid* DORIAS
　　returns from THRASO'S *carrying* THAIS' *jewellery.*]

DORIAS: Heaven help me, from what I've seen of that man
　I'll swear he's mad! I'm terrified he'll make a scene and do
　Thais an injury. When young Chremes turned up, the
　girl's brother, she asked Thraso to invite him in. That put
　him in a temper at once, but he didn't dare refuse, and
　Thais went on pressing him. Her object was to keep
　Chremes there, for it wasn't the right moment to tell him
　all she wanted about his sister. Thraso asked him in with a
　bad grace; Chremes stayed, and Thais immediately began
　to talk to him. Thraso imagined she'd brought in a rival
　under his very nose, so to pay her back he told a boy to
　fetch Pamphila 'to amuse us'. 'That girl at a dinner-party?'
　said Thais: 'Certainly not.' Thraso insisted, and they had
　words. Then Thais removed her jewels unperceived and
　gave them to me to take away. I know what this means – as
　soon as she can she'll slip away from the party.

　　[*She is about to go into* THAIS' *house when* PHAEDRIA
　　comes on from the left.]

PHAEDRIA: On my way out to the country I began to think
　of this and that, always looking on the gloomy side, as you
　do when there's something weighing on your mind, and to
　cut a long story short, I passed our farm without seeing it –
　I'd gone a long way before I noticed. I went back, annoyed
　with myself, but when I reached the turning I stopped and
　began thinking again. 'Must I really spend two days alone
　here without her? And then what? I suppose it doesn't
　matter . . . but it does. . . . There's no chance of being with
　her but at least I could *see* her – that'll be allowed. Love at a

distance is better than nothing.' So this time I passed the house deliberately. [PYTHIAS *bursts out of* THAIS' *house.* Now why the devil is Pythias rushing out in such a state?

PYTHIAS: Where is he? Brute, monster, where can he be? Oh to think he could dare to do such a wicked thing!

PHAEDRIA: Good lord, this sounds bad.

PYTHIAS: And to add insult to injury, after he'd wronged the girl he tore her frock and pulled the poor thing's hair!

PHAEDRIA: What!

PYTHIAS: Just let me get my hands on him – I'd scratch his eyes out, the poisonous snake!

PHAEDRIA: Something awful must have happened while I was away. I'll go and ask her. Pythias, what's all this? What's the hurry? Who is it you want?

PYTHIAS [*coldly*]: Phaedria! Need you ask? You go to hell – the proper place for you *and* your fine presents.

PHAEDRIA: What on earth do you mean?

PYTHIAS: You know very well. That eunuch you gave us – Oh, what a mess we're in! And the girl, the one Thraso gave my mistress – he's had her.

PHAEDRIA: What!

PYTHIAS: Oh it's terrible!

PHAEDRIA: Nonsense, you're drunk.

PYTHIAS: Drunk? I only wish my enemies felt like I do.

DORIAS: My dear Pythias, you must explain how – it's fantastic.

PHAEDRIA: You're crazy. *How* could a eunuch –

PYTHIAS: Don't ask me how: but it's quite clear that he did. The girl does nothing but cry and can't bring herself to answer any questions. The man has vanished; so much for his honesty. And oh dear me, I'm sure he's gone off with something from the house.

PHAEDRIA: I'd be surprised if he's gone far, a poor creature like him. He's probably gone back to our house.

PYTHIAS: Then do please go and see. [PHAEDRIA *goes into* LACHES' *house*.]

DORIAS: My conscience, it's monstrous! My dear, I never heard of such a thing!

PYTHIAS: Well, I've always been told their type falls heavily for women, but they can't. . . . It certainly never crossed my mind – or I'd have shut him up and never trusted him with the girl.

　　[PHAEDRIA *returns, dragging* DORUS *dressed in* CHAEREA'S *clothes*.]

PHAEDRIA: Come out, you scoundrel! Still trying to clear off, are you? Come *on*, you rotten bargain!

DORUS: Please, Sir.

PHAEDRIA: Look at the face he's pulled, the brute! What do you mean, going back like that and changing your clothes? Come on, answer. If I'd waited another minute, Pythias, I'd have missed him – he'd already planned his escape.

PYTHIAS [*mystified*]: Have you caught him, Sir?

PHAEDRIA: Of course I have.

PYTHIAS: Well done!

DORIAS: Oh, how splendid!

PYTHIAS: Where is he?

PHAEDRIA: What do you mean? Can't you see him?

PYTHIAS: See who, please?

PHAEDRIA: This man, of course.

PYTHIAS: Who's *he*?

PHAEDRIA: He was brought over to you only today.

PYTHIAS: But none of us have ever set eyes on him, Sir.

PHAEDRIA: What!

PYTHIAS: Did you suppose *this* was the man who was brought to us?

PHAEDRIA: I had no one else to send.

PYTHIAS: But there's no comparison! The other one was gentlemanly and good looking.

PHAEDRIA: He only seemed so then because he was smartened up in coloured clothes. He cuts a poor figure now because he hasn't got them.

PYTHIAS: Nonsense, there's more to it than that. The man brought to us today was young; you'd have found him a pleasure to the eye yourself, Sir. This is a worn-out, wrinkled, senile old man, the colour of a weasel.

PHAEDRIA: Damn it all, what are you saying? Are you trying to make out that I'm not responsible for my actions? [To DORUS] Here you, did I buy you?

DORUS: Yes, Sir, you did.

PYTHIAS: Now tell him to answer *me* a question.

PHAEDRIA: Go on then.

PYTHIAS: Did you come to our house today? [DORUS *shakes his head*] He says No. But someone else did, a lad of sixteen, brought by Parmeno.

PHAEDRIA: Let's get this clear first; where did you get those clothes you are wearing? Come on, answer. You dumb brute, can't you speak?

DORUS: Chaerea came –

PHAEDRIA: My brother?

DORUS: Yes.

PHAEDRIA: When?

DORUS: Today.

PHAEDRIA: How long ago?

DORUS: Just now.

PHAEDRIA: Anyone with him?

DORUS: Parmeno.

PHAEDRIA: Had you seen him before?

DORUS: No, I'd never even heard of him.

PHAEDRIA: Then how did you know he was my brother?

DORUS: Parmeno said so. Your brother gave me these clothes —

PHAEDRIA: Damn it!

DORUS: And he put on mine. Then they left the house together.

PYTHIAS: *Now* will you believe I'm not drunk? I told you the sober truth. Does this convince you now what happened to the girl?

PHAEDRIA [*reluctantly*]: Come, come, look at the creature; do you believe what *he* says?

PYTHIAS: No need to believe him. The facts speak for themselves.

PHAEDRIA [*to* DORUS]: Just come over here a little; do you hear? A little further — that'll do. Now tell me again: Chaerea took your clothes —

DORUS: That's right.

PHAEDRIA: — and put them on —

DORUS: Right.

PHAEDRIA: — and was taken to that house in your place?

DORUS: Yes.

PHAEDRIA: Good God, the wanton impudence of the boy!

PYTHIAS (*crying*): Oh, it was a wicked trick to play on us! Can't you believe me now?

PHAEDRIA: Oh, you'd believe anything he says. [*Aside*] What am I to do? [*To* DORUS] Now this time answer No. [*Aloud*] I'll drag the truth out of you here and now! *Did* you see my brother Chaerea?

DORUS: No.

PHAEDRIA: He can't tell the truth without torture, I can see. Come along with me. First he says Yes, then No. [*Aside to* DORUS] Beg for mercy.

DORUS: Please, please, Sir. . . .

PHAEDRIA [*kicking him into the house*]: Go in at once.

[DORUS *goes in with a howl of pain.*]

PHAEDRIA [*aside*]: How else can I get out of this without losing face? [*Shouts into the house*] If you still try fooling me, you scoundrel – you're for it. [*He follows* DORUS *into the house.*]

PYTHIAS: Sure as I live, this is one of Parmeno's tricks.

DORIAS: It must be.

PYTHIAS: I'll find some way to pay him back. What do you think we ought to do, Dorias?

DORIAS: About the girl, do you mean?

PYTHIAS: Yes. Shall I mention it or keep my mouth shut?

DORIAS: Why, if you're wise you'll know nothing about the eunuch and what happened to the girl. That'll keep you out of all this trouble and win her gratitude. All you need say is that Dorus has run off.

PYTHIAS: All right, I will.

DORIAS [*looking down street, right*]: Look, there's Chremes. Thais'll be here soon.

PYTHIAS: What makes you think so?

DORIAS: A quarrel had broken out at Thraso's when I left.

PYTHIAS: You go and put away those jewels. I'll find out from him what's happening.

[DORIAS *goes in.* CHREMES *comes on from the right, rather drunk.*]

CHREMES: It's a cheat . . . and a swindle. . . . Damn it all, I'm drunk. So long as I sat still I seemed nice and sober. . . . Then I got up . . . head's all wrong . . . [*staggers*] legs too. . . .

PYTHIAS: Chremes!

CHREMES: Who's there? Pythias! You're a beauty . . . lovelier than ever!

PYTHIAS [*primly*]: You're the merrier, Sir, no doubt about that.

CHREMES: Well, it's true. . . . 'Love needs a bite and a sup to warm things up.' . . . Thais been back long?

PYTHIAS: Has she left the party already?

CHREMES: Long ago . . . ages ago. . . . There was a simply terrific row.

PYTHIAS: But didn't she tell you to follow her?

CHREMES: All she did . . . was give me . . . a bit of a nod . . . as she left.

PYTHIAS: And wasn't that enough for you?

CHREMES: I didn't know what she meant . . . till Thraso put me right . . . and kicked me out. Here she is. . . . I wonder where I got ahead of her.

[THAIS *comes on right with her two maids.*]

THAIS: He'll be here in a minute, I suppose, to take Pamphila from me. Just let him try! If he lays a finger on her I'll scratch his eyes out! I can put up with his stupid ways and bragging words as long as they *are* words, but if it comes to actions, I'll have him horse-whipped!

CHREMES: Thais, I've been here a long time.

THAIS: Chremes my dear, I was looking for you. Do you realize that you're the cause of this scene? None of it would have started but for you.

CHREMES: Me? what are you talking about?

THAIS: It was my eagerness to restore your sister to your keeping that brought all this on my head, and a lot more besides.

CHREMES: Where is she?

THAIS: In my house.

CHREMES: What!

THAIS: Don't worry, I've looked after her – I've done the right thing by you both.

CHREMES: Really?

THAIS: Truly. I'm making you a present of her, and I don't expect a penny in return.

CHREMES [*stiffly*]: Then I can only repay you by my proper gratitude, Thais.

THAIS: But watch out, or you'll lose her before you receive her from me; she's the girl Thraso is coming to carry off by force. Pythias, you go and fetch the little box with the proofs.

CHREMES: Look, he's coming –

PYTHIAS [*to* THAIS]: Where is it?

THAIS: In the chest. Oh do *hurry*!

CHREMES: Good God, look at the army he's bringing!

THAIS: My dear man, you're not afraid are you?

CHREMES [*visibly alarmed*]: Nonsense. Who's afraid? Not me

THAIS: That's the spirit.

CHREMES: What do you take me for, I should like to know

THAIS: All right, I only want you to remember that you're dealing with a foreigner who is less influential and wel known than you are, with fewer friends in Athens.

CHREMES: Yes, I know all that, but it's silly to sit dowr under things you can avoid. I'd rather take preventive action than have to retaliate after damage is done. You go in and bolt the door while I run and bring help – we'll need it against what's coming to us.

THAIS: Stay here –

CHREMES: No, better not.

THAIS [*holding on to him*]: No, stay.

CHREMES: Let go; I'll soon be back.

THAIS: But it's quite unnecessary, Chremes. All you need dc is to tell him she is the sister you lost when she was small and now you've recognized her. [*To* PYTHIAS *as she comes out with the box*] Show him the proofs.

PYTHIAS: Here they are.

THAIS: Take them. If he shows violence you can always give him in charge. Do you understand?

CHREMES [*dubiously*]: I suppose so.

THAIS: You must be firm with him.

CHREMES: I will. . . .

THAIS: Prepare yourself for battle. [*Aside*] Good heavens, I'm lost. What a man to defend me! He needs a champion of his own.

[*They all go into the house as* THRASO *marches on right with* GNATHO *and a motley band of followers – six in all.*]

THRASO: Am I to put up with such a deliberate insult, Gnatho? Better death than dishonour! Simalio, Donax, Syriscus, follow me. First I'll storm the house.

GNATHO: Right, Sir.

THRASO: I'll carry off the girl.

GNATHO: Very good, Sir.

THRASO: And then I'll punish that female.

GNATHO: Splendid, Sir.

THRASO: Centre here, Donax, with the crowbar. Simalio, on the left wing. Syriscus, you on the right. Bring up the reserves. Where's Sergeant Sanga and his kitchen squad of thieves?

SANGA [*stepping forward*]: Present, Sir.

THRASO: What's that, you fool? Do you propose to fight a battle with that sponge you're carrying?

SANGA: Sir? I know my general's valour and the army's spirit. There's bound to be bloodshed, said I; I'll need something to staunch their wounds.

THRASO: Where are the others?

SANGA: What others, damn it? There's only Sannio left on guard at home.

THRASO [*to* GNATHO]: Draw them up. I'll take up my position behind the front line; from there I'll give the order to them all.

GNATHO: Sound tactics! [*Aside*] A formation designed to giv
him a safe place.

THRASO [*complacently*]: I am only following Pyrrhus' practice
[CHREMES *and* THAIS *appear at a window.*]

CHREMES: Look what he's doing, Thais. You see I was righ
about bolting the door.

THAIS: I can see the man's a coward, though you may thin]
him a hero. You needn't be afraid of *him*.

THRASO: Well, what now?

GNATHO: I was just wishing you had one of those big siege-
engines so that you could pick them off from a distance
unseen; that would rout the lot.

THRASO: Look there – isn't that Thais?

GNATHO: How soon do we attack?

THRASO: Wait. A wise man should try everything before h
has recourse to arms. For all you know I may get my owi
way with her without using force.

GNATHO: Heavens above, what wisdom! Every minute spen
with you is something learned.

THRASO: Thais, first answer me this: when I gave you th
girl, did you promise to keep the next few days for m
alone?

THAIS: What if I did?

THRASO: Can you ask – when you have brought your love
into my presence, under my very nose?

THAIS: What's that to you?

THRASO: And slipped off with him when I wasn't looking:

THAIS: Well, I wanted to.

THRASO: All right. Now give back Pamphila, unless you'
rather I took her by force.

CHREMES: Give her back! If you so much as lay a finger o]
her, you –

GNATHO: Just you shut up!

THRASO: What's that? Can't I lay hands on my own property?

CHREMES: *Your* property, you dirty brute?

GNATHO: Please be careful. You don't know the man you're insulting.

CHREMES [*to* GNATHO]: You clear off! [*To* THRASO] Do you realize what you're letting yourself in for? If you make any move to cause trouble here today, I'll give you something to make you remember the place and time – and me – for ever.

GNATHO: You're trying to make an enemy out of this gentleman; well, I'm sorry for you.

CHREMES: Clear off, or I'll break your head!

GNATHO: Really? So that's the way you carry on, you swine?

THRASO: Who do you think you are, and what do you want? What interest have you in the girl?

CHREMES: Listen. In the first place I can tell you she is free born.

THRASO: What!

CHREMES: – a citizen of Attica –

THRASO: No!

CHREMES: – and my sister.

THRASO: What barefaced impudence!

CHREMES: I'm just giving you warning, Thraso, not to use any force on her. Thais, I'm going to fetch the nurse Sophrona and show her the proofs.

THRASO: Are you trying to stop me from laying hands on my own property?

CHREMES: I'll stop you all right.

[*He leaves the window, comes out of the house, and walks off right in triumph.*]

GNATHO: Did you hear that? He proves himself guilty of theft. That's all the evidence you need.

THRASO: Do you agree with that, Thais?

THAIS: Find someone else to answer you. [*She slams the window shut.*]

THRASO: Now what do we do?

GNATHO: Go home. She'll soon come round of her own accord and eat humble pie.

THRASO: Do you really think so?

GNATHO: Of course I do. I know women and their ways. Whatever you want, they won't have, and then set their hearts on it after you've given up.

THRASO: I suppose you're right.

GNATHO: May I tell the men to fall out?

THRASO: When you like.

GNATHO: Sanga, the moment has come to take thought of hearth and home, as a true soldier should.

SANGA: My mind's been on my saucepans this long while.

GNATHO: Good fellow.

THRASO: Follow me, my men.

[*They march off right. When they have gone,* THAIS *and* PYTHIAS *come out of the house.*]

THAIS: You wretched woman, can't you stop talking in riddles? 'I know – I don't know – he ran off – they said – he wasn't there –' If you've anything to tell me, can't you speak plainly? The girl's dress is torn, she does nothing but cry and won't say a word. The eunuch has vanished. Why? What has happened? Can't you speak?

PYTHIAS: Oh dear, where can I begin? They say he wasn't the eunuch –

THAIS: Who was he then?

PYTHIAS: That Chaerea –

THAIS: What Chaerea?

PYTHIAS: That young brother of Phaedria's.

THAIS: Nonsense, you scandal-monger.

PYTHIAS: It's true. I proved it.

HAIS: What on earth did he want with us? Why was he taken to my house?

YTHIAS: I don't know, but I suppose he's in love with Pamphila.

HAIS: Oh I shall die of shame, you miserable creature, if there's any truth in what you say. Is *that* why the girl is crying?

YTHIAS: I think so.

HAIS: Impossible, you liar. Wasn't that the very thing I warned you against when I went out?

YTHIAS: What was I to do? I did as you told me yourself and gave him sole charge of her.

HAIS: You fool, it was trusting the wolf with the lamb. Oh, I'm so ashamed of being taken in like this! What sort of a man can he be?

YTHIAS [*eagerly*]: Madam, please, say no more; we're saved. There's our man.

HAIS: Where?

YTHIAS: Look left; can't you see him coming?

HAIS: Yes.

YTHIAS: Have him arrested at once.

HAIS: What are we to do with him, you fool?

YTHIAS: Need you ask? Now look carefully, Madam, when he comes in sight and see if he hasn't a bold face. [CHAEREA *comes on from the right still wearing the eunuch's clothes.*] Am I right? The impudence of the man!

HAEREA: Well, I went to Antipho's, but both his parents were there as if they'd stayed at home on purpose, so I couldn't go in without them seeing me. Then when I was standing outside the door someone I knew came along and I had to take to my heels as fast as I could down an empty alley, and make my escape from one to another in agonies all the time for fear someone would recognize me. But

that must be Thais I can see – yes, it is. That's torn it
What'll happen now? What will she do to me?

THAIS: Let's meet him. Dorus, my man, here you are. Now
tell me: have you been trying to escape?

CHAEREA: That's right, Madam.

THAIS: And you congratulate yourself on doing so?

CHAEREA: No, Madam.

THAIS: Do you expect to go unpunished?

CHAEREA: Please overlook this one lapse, Madam. If I ever
do wrong again you can kill me.

THAIS: It wasn't because you were afraid I'd be a cruel
mistress?

CHAEREA: No, Madam.

THAIS: Then what was it?

CHAEREA [*indicating* PYTHIAS]: Her. I was afraid she'd go to
you complaining about me.

THAIS: What had you done?

CHAEREA: Nothing much.

PYTHIAS: Nothing much! Have you no shame? Do you call
it 'nothing much' to assault a virgin and a free-born
citizen?

CHAEREA: I took her for a fellow slave.

PYTHIAS: Fellow slave! I can scarcely keep my hands off your
hair, you brute! And now he's come to laugh over us.

THAIS: You're beside yourself; leave us.

PYTHIAS: What? I suppose I'd be the one to pay damages if I
got at him, the beast – and all the more since he was only
pretending to be your slave.

THAIS: Pythias, this must stop. Chaerea, your conduct was
unworthy of you. Even if it were right for me to be insulted
like this, it was quite wrong for you to behave in this way. I
have no idea what I can best do for this girl – you have
thoroughly upset all my plans. It's impossible for me to do

the right thing now and hand her back to her family as I was anxious to do. I could also have gained some solid advantage for myself.

HAEREA: But I'm hoping that from now on there will be a lasting bond of good feeling between us, Thais. It often happens in a situation like this that a bad start leads to a close friendship. It may, in fact, be heaven's will.

HAIS [*after a pause*]: Well. . . . I am willing to look at it that way myself.

HAEREA: Please do. And there's just one thing I should like you to know – I hadn't any intention of insulting you. I did it for love of her.

HAIS: I realize that, Chaerea, and it makes me all the more ready to forgive you. I'm not altogether lacking in human feeling or experience; I know something of the power of love.

HAEREA: I swear to God I love you too, Thais.

YTHIAS: In that case, Madam, I fancy you'd better watch out on your own account.

HAEREA: I wouldn't dare –

YTHIAS: I don't trust you an inch.

HAIS [*laughing*]: Be quiet!

HAEREA: Now let me beg you to help me in this, Thais. I put myself in your hands with complete confidence in your discretion. Be my protector, hear my prayers – I shall die if I can't marry her.

HAIS: What about your father?

HAEREA: Him? Oh he'll be willing enough I'm sure – if only she were a free citizen.

HAIS: If you'll just wait a little her brother will be here himself. He went to fetch the nurse who looked after her as a child. Then you can be present at the recognition.

HAEREA: Of course I'll wait.

THAIS: Meanwhile, would you like to wait for him indoor instead of standing here in the street?

CHAEREA: I'd like nothing better.

PYTHIAS: *Now* what are you up to, Madam?

THAIS: What *is* the matter?

PYTHIAS: Need you ask? Do you really intend to receive thi man in your house after what has happened?

THAIS: Why not?

PYTHIAS: Mark my words, he'll make fresh trouble.

THAIS: Hold your tongue, I say.

PYTHIAS: You can't have seen through his bold front.

CHAEREA: I shan't do anything, Pythias.

PYTHIAS: I should have to be sure what you haven't done before I trust you, Chaerea.

CHAEREA: Well then, you can keep an eye on me.

PYTHIAS: Get along with you; I'd no more dare to look afte you than give you something to look after.

THAIS [*looking down the street*]: Ah, splendid; here comes he brother.

CHAEREA: Oh no, please, Thais, do let's go indoors – I don' want him to see me in the street in these clothes.

THAIS [*amused*]: Why not? Are you bashful?

CHAEREA: Yes I am.

PYTHIAS: Really? Spare his maiden blushes!

THAIS: Go in, I'll follow. Wait here, Pythias, to let Chreme in.

[*She follows* CHAEREA *into the house.*]

PYTHIAS: Oh if I could only think of something – some way of paying back that scoundrel who planted this man on us

[CHREMES *comes on right, with the old nurse,* SOPHRONA.

CHREMES: Do get a move on, nurse.

SOPHRONA: I am moving.

CHREMES: I can see you are, but you don't move *on*.

PYTHIAS: Have you shown her the proofs yet?

CHREMES: Yes, every one.

PYTHIAS: Please, what did she say? Did she recognize them?

CHREMES: Perfectly.

PYTHIAS: That's good news! I'm fond of the girl. Go in – the mistress has been waiting for you for ages. [*They go in.*] And now here comes our worthy friend Parmeno, sauntering along without a care in the world! Please heaven, I believe I've thought up a way of tormenting him. I'll just pop indoors to make sure of the recognition scene and then be back to terrify the life out of him for his wicked lies. [*She goes in.*]

   [PARMENO *comes on right, looking pleased with himself.*]

PARMENO: Here I am again, to see how Chaerea's getting on. If he's played his cards well, my God, what glory for me – and rightly. To say nothing of the satisfactory consummation I have procured without trouble or expense of any kind in a love affair which might have proved difficult and costly, as the girl was in the power of a greedy professional – there is this further achievement, which I consider my real masterpiece: I have found a way of giving a young man a glimpse of the character and habits of loose women early in life, so that the lesson learned in time will make him hate them for ever. Met outside their own homes, dining with a lover and pecking daintily at their food, these women give an impression of perfect elegance, composure, and good taste; but just see the sordid filth and squalor and their nasty habits and greed when they're at home by themselves, gobbling up black bread soaked in yesterday's soup – to know all this is a young man's salvation.

PYTHIAS [*who has come out again in time to hear some of this*]: I'll see you suffer for these words, you brute, and for what

you've done too – you shan't get away with fooling us.
[*Raising her voice but still ignoring* PARMENO] Heavens above,
what a wicked deed! Oh the poor young man! Oh that
vile Parmeno who brought him here!

PARMENO: What's that?

PYTHIAS: I'm sorry for him. . . . I couldn't bear it, I came out
here so as not to see the cruel punishment they say he's
going to suffer.

PARMENO: Good God, what's all this? It can't mean trouble
for me. . . . I'll ask her. What's the matter, Pythias? What
are you saying? Who's going to be punished?

PYTHIAS: Need you ask, impudence? You brought a young
man here instead of the eunuch; all you think about is
tricking us, but you've been the death of *him*.

PARMENO: How? What happened? Go on.

PYTHIAS: I'll tell you. That girl who was given to Thais
today – did you realize she's a free-born citizen? And has a
brother in one of the best families?

PARMENO [*uncomfortably*]: I don't know, I'm sure.

PYTHIAS: Well, that's what's come out. Your wretched fellow
assaulted her, and when her brother found out, in a proper
fury –

PARMENO: What did he do?

PYTHIAS: First he tied him up in a shocking fashion –

PARMENO: Tied him up?

PYTHIAS: Yes, though Thais begged him not to.

PARMENO: Impossible!

PYTHIAS: And now he's threatening to deal with him as they
do adulterers – a thing I've never seen and shouldn't want
to see.

PARMENO [*horrified*]: How could he dare to do such a monstrous thing!

PYTHIAS: Why monstrous?

PARMENO: Could it be worse? And whoever saw a man arrested for adultery in a house of this reputation?

PYTHIAS [*imitating him*]: I don't know, I'm sure.

PARMENO: But I'll have you all know this, Pythias – and be warned. I tell you this young man is my master's son.

PYTHIAS: Gracious, you don't say so!

PARMENO: Thais had better not let anything happen to him. I think I'd best go in myself. [*He moves towards* THAIS' *house.*]

PYTHIAS [*catching at him*]: Be careful what you're doing, Parmeno: you may do him no good and yourself harm. They think you were at the bottom of everything that happened.

PARMENO: What on earth am I to do then? Where am I to start? [*Looking along the street.*] And now here's my old master coming back from the country. Shall I tell him or not? Better tell him – even if it means trouble for me, I must help the boy.

PYTHIAS: You're right. I'm going in; you tell him the whole story.

[*She goes into the house as the young men's father,* LACHES, *comes on left.*]

LACHES: There's one advantage in having a country place so near town: I'm never bored in either place. When I've had enough of one I can change to the other. But isn't that our man Parmeno? Yes, it is. Parmeno! Why are you standing outside this door? Are you waiting for someone?

PARMENO [*jumps round*]: Who's that? Oh, Sir, I'm glad to see you safely back.

LACHES: Who is it you're waiting for?

PARMENO [*aside*]: Damn it, I'm struck dumb with fear.

LACHES: Well, what is it? You're shaking – aren't you well? Speak up.

PARMENO: Sir, I'd like you first to know the facts; whatever
happened here, it wasn't my fault.

LACHES: What did happen?

PARMENO: Quite right, Sir, I should have told you that first.
Phaedria bought a eunuch to give to – the lady here.

LACHES: Who's she?

PARMENO: Thais.

LACHES: He *bought* one? That'll finish me. How much?

PARMENO: Two thousand drachmas.

LACHES: I'm ruined.

PARMENO: Then Chaerea's having an affair with a girl in this
house –

LACHES: *What!* Chaerea having an affair? What does he
know about those women at his age? Is he in town? One
trouble leads to another!

PARMENO: Don't look at me like that, Sir, please; I didn't
put him up to it.

LACHES: Never mind about that. I'll see to *you*, you scoundrel,
if this doesn't kill me. First you tell me what you're trying
to say.

PARMENO: Chaerea was taken to Thais instead of the
eunuch –

LACHES: Instead of a *eunuch*?

PARMENO: Yes. And afterwards . . . they arrested him as an
adulterer and tied him up.

LACHES: Oh no, no!

PARMENO: It just shows the impudence of these women,
Sir.

LACHES [*after a shocked pause*]: Is there any other disaster or
disgrace I haven't heard?

PARMENO: That's the lot, Sir.

LACHES: Then I shall go straight in. [*He rushes into* THAIS'
house.]

ARMENO: That spells trouble for me as well, no doubt about it. Well, it can't be helped, and anyway I'm glad I've made trouble for those bitches too. The old man has been looking for an excuse for ages to do something drastic to them, and now he's found one.

[PYTHIAS *comes out, laughing.*]

PYTHIAS: That's the best thing I could have wanted to happen! Oh the way old Laches burst in on us, barking up the wrong tree! I'd the joke to myself – no one else knew what he dreaded to see.

ARMENO [*aside*]: *Now* what's happened?

PYTHIAS: I must find Parmeno! Where on earth is he?

ARMENO [*aside*]: She wants *me*.

PYTHIAS: There he is, I'll – [*Goes on laughing.*]

ARMENO: What's the matter, you fool? What do you want? What are you laughing about? Can't you stop?

PYTHIAS: This'll be the death of me! I've split my sides laughing at you.

ARMENO: Why?

PYTHIAS: Don't you know? A sillier man I've never seen and never shall see! Oh I can't tell you what fun you've given us indoors – and I used to think you such a smart clever fellow! Did you have to swallow whole the tale I just told you? You ought to be ashamed of putting young Chaerea up to the shocking things he did, without giving the poor boy away to his father. What do you suppose the old man felt when he saw his son in those clothes? Well – now do you believe you're done for?

ARMENO: What's that you say, you wretched woman? Did you make up that tale? You're still laughing – do you find it funny to fool us?

PYTHIAS: Very funny [*laughs still more*].

ARMENO: If you get out of this for nothing –

PYTHIAS: Well?

PARMENO: I'll pay you out, I swear I will.

PYTHIAS: I don't doubt it, Parmeno, but maybe your threats
have to wait for another day – and meanwhile you'll han[g]
for ruining the character of a silly boy and then telling o[n]
him; father and son will both make an example of you.

PARMENO: It's the end.

PYTHIAS: It's your reward for faithful service. Good-by[e]
[*She goes in, laughing.*]

PARMENO: Damn it all, it's my own fault – betrayed like [a]
mouse with my own squeaking.

[THRASO *and* GNATHO *come on from the right.*]

GNATHO: What are you proposing now, Thraso? What d[o]
you hope to gain by coming back here? What are yo[u]
trying to do?

THRASO [*impressively*]: I shall surrender myself to Thais an[d]
do her bidding.

GNATHO: What!

THRASO: Why not? Hercules turned slave to Omphale.

GNATHO: Ah yes, a noble precedent. [*Aside*] I hope I'll se[e]
her take a slipper to knock your head into shape. [*T[o]*
THRASO] I can hear her door opening.

[CHAEREA *bursts out, in his own clothes, wildly excite[d]*
THRASO *and* GNATHO *stand aside.*]

THRASO: Good God, more trouble! Who's this? I've neve[r]
seen him in my life. Why's he rushing out in such [a]
hurry?

CHAEREA: Good people all, is there a man alive as lucky as [I]
am? No one, I'll swear. So much has turned out well fo[r]
me so quickly, and all the powers of heaven are on my side[.]

PARMENO: Now why's he so pleased with himself?

CHAEREA [*seeing* PARMENO *and hugging him*]: Parmeno[,]
dear man, author and instigator and perfecter of all m[y]

joys, do you know how happy I am? Do you realize my
Pamphila turns out to be a free citizen?

PARMENO: I'd heard that.

CHAEREA: And I'm going to marry her?

PARMENO: *That* will be a deed well done.

GNATHO [*to* THRASO]: Did you hear that?

CHAEREA: And then I'm so happy for my brother – Phaedria's love affair has weathered its storms, and we're going
to be one happy family. Thais has found favour with
my father and has put herself entirely under our protection.

PARMENO: So she's all your brother's?

CHAEREA: Evidently.

PARMENO: Then there's another cause for rejoicing – Thraso
will be kicked out.

CHAEREA [*shaking him*]: Quick, quick, find my brother and
tell him at once.

PARMENO: I'll see if he's at home [*goes into* LACHES' *house*].

THRASO: Gnatho, I suppose there's no doubt this finishes me
for good and all?

GNATHO: No doubt at all, I fancy.

CHAEREA: Where shall I begin? Who deserves most praise?
Parmeno who gave me the idea, or myself who dared to
carry it out? Or should it be Fortune who guided me and
brought so many vital matters to a happy conclusion in a
single day? Or my father for his kindness and good humour?
All I pray is that heaven's blessing will continue!

[PHAEDRIA *hurries out of Laches' house.*]

PHAEDRIA: Good lord, this is a fantastic story! Where's my
brother?

CHAEREA: Here he is.

PHAEDRIA: I'm delighted.

CHAEREA: I'm sure you are. No one deserves your love more

than your Thais, Phaedria; she has done so much for all
our family.

PHAEDRIA [*laughing*]: I don't need you to praise Thais!

THRASO: Damn it, the fainter my hopes the more I love her.
Please, Gnatho, I pin all my hopes on you.

GNATHO: What do you want me to do?

THRASO: Beg him – or pay him – to let me keep on some
sort of footing with Thais.

GNATHO: It won't be easy.

THRASO: If you really want something – I know you. Only
manage this, and you can ask for any reward you like; you
shall have it.

GNATHO: Do you mean that?

THRASO: I do.

GNATHO: If I succeed I'll ask for your house to be open to
me whether you're at home or not, then I need never
wait for an invitation and can always be sure of a place.

THRASO: I give you my word on that.

GNATHO: Then I'll prepare myself for battle. [*They move up
to the others.*]

PHAEDRIA: Who's that? Oh, good evening, Thraso.

THRASO: Good evening to you both.

PHAEDRIA: Perhaps you haven't heard what has been happening here?

THRASO: I know.

PHAEDRIA: Then why do I see you round here at all?

THRASO: I was relying on you –

PHAEDRIA: Shall I tell you what you *can* rely on? Listen to
me, my man; if I ever find you in this street again, even if
you tell me you just happen to be passing through looking
for someone else – you're a dead man.

GNATHO: This is no way to talk!

PHAEDRIA: That's all I have to say.

THRASO: I can't understand your attitude –

PHAEDRIA: I mean it.

GNATHO: Let me say a few words first, and when you've heard me you can carry on if you like.

CHAEREA: Let's hear him.

GNATHO: Just move off a little way over there, Thraso. [*To the others*] Now first of all, I very much want you to understand that all I'm doing is primarily in my own interests; but if it happens to benefit you too, it would be silly of you not to fall in with it.

PHAEDRIA: Well, what is it?

GNATHO: In my opinion you should accept Thraso as a rival.

PHAEDRIA: What! Accept him –

GNATHO: Now think, Phaedria; for you to go on enjoying life with Thais, living in the style you do, you must always be paying out to her, and you haven't really much to give. Thraso's the man to provide for all the requirements of love without it costing you a penny – no one can be so useful. In the first place, he has the means and he's lavish with his money. Then he's a silly idiot, a dim-wit who snores night and day; you need never fear any woman will fall for him, and you can easily throw him out when you like.

CHAEREA [*to* PHAEDRIA]: What shall we do?

GNATHO: Then there's what I consider more important than anything; no one entertains so well on the scale he does.

CHAEREA: It looks as though we need the man after all.

PHAEDRIA [*reluctantly*]: I suppose so.

GNATHO: Thank you. Now there's just one more thing – please let me into your circle. I've had uphill work long enough with that clod.

PHAEDRIA: All right, we will.

CHAEREA: With pleasure.

GNATHO: In return I offer you both – Thraso: for the laughs and everything else you can get out of him.

CHAEREA: We'll take him.

PHAEDRIA: He deserves it.

GNATHO: Thraso, you can come here now.

THRASO [*coming across*]: For pity's sake, how are we getting on?

GNATHO [*airily*]: Oh they didn't know you; I only had to reveal your true character and praise you according to your deeds and merits, and it was easy.

THRASO: Splendid. I'm most grateful. [*Recovering his complacency*] I must say I've always found myself exceedingly popular wherever I've been.

GNATHO [*to* PHAEDRIA *and* CHAEREA]: Perfect taste, as I told you!

PHAEDRIA [*laughing*]: Up to expectations anyway! This way, please.

[*They all go into* THAIS' *house.*]

The Mother-in-Law

[HECYRA]

INTRODUCTORY NOTE

The Mother-in-Law is generally considered to be Terence's fifth play, but there are indications that it was written earlier, and that its final successful production was after *The Brothers*. The two production notices and the discrepancy between Donatus and the production notice on the subject of its Greek model point to recollections of different productions. It must have been a play which Terence and his producer valued, or they would not have persisted in reviving it after two failures. It is certainly Terence's most original play, with its close-knit plot, absence of comic fooling, clearly defined characterization, and economy of dialogue pruned down to a mere 880 lines. It has always won admiration, and critics have judged it to be the prototype of serious domestic comedy.

The problem is a common one: a marriage is breaking down and the two families involved are trying to save it. Everyone is acting for the best, but the comedy arises out of the fact that the truth of the situation is withheld even from the audience until the final scene. So the young man's harassed father vents his feelings on his wife, and she is prepared to leave home if it will help towards a reconciliation. The girl's mother stands by her daughter and adds to the confusion by trying to conceal things from her husband. The young wife, though never seen, becomes a personality through what different people say about her, and her young husband's character is sympathetically drawn in depth, his self-pity in his first scene being ousted by a new restraint and consideration for others when he is confronted by a real crisis. Throughout Terence observes people's reactions to an unforeseen situation with a good deal of quiet humour – the two fathers' delight in a grandchild and the new problem presented to Pamphilus thereby, and Bacchis' calm mastery of her scene with Laches contain some of the best passages he ever wrote.

This is a play in which the women provide the chief interest – the two mothers, the girl, and especially the courtesan Bacchis, whose charm and dignity are shown by contrast with Laches' clumsy approach and Pamphilus' youthful self-centredness, as well as by the vulgarity of the pair in the opening scene who lead us to expect someone quite different.

PRODUCTION NOTICE I

THE MOTHER-IN-LAW by Terence: performed at the Megalesian Games during the curule aedileship of Sextus Julius Caesar and Gnaeus Dolobella.[1]

Music composed by Flaccus, slave of Claudius, for a pair of pipes throughout.

Greek original by Menander.

The author's fifth play.

First performance without a prologue.

Second performance during the consulship of Gnaeus Octavius and Titus Manlius, at the funeral games for Lucius Aemilius Paulus:[2] a failure.

Third performance during the aedileship of Quintus Fulvius and Lucius Marcius, produced by Lucius Ambivius and Lucius Sergius Turpio: a success.[3]

1. i.e. 165 B.C.
2. i.e. 160 B.C. L. A. Paullus Macedonicus was the father of Scipio Aemilianus who was adopted into the Scipio family. See p. 9. The incorrect spelling appears in all the Production Notices.
3. Also in 160 B.C.

PRODUCTION NOTICE II

THE MOTHER-IN-LAW by Terence: performed at the Roman Games[1] during the curule aedileship of Sextus Julius Caesar and Gnaeus Cornelius, but withdrawn unfinished.

Music composed by Flaccus, slave of Claudius, for a pair of pipes throughout.

Second performance during the consulship of Gnaeus Octavius and Titus Manlius, at the funeral games for Lucius Aemilius Paulus.

Third performance during the aedileship of Quintus Fulvius and Lucius Martius.

1. Held annually on 4 September in honour of Jupiter.

SYNOPSIS

Pamphilus marries Philumena not knowing that she is the girl he once assaulted, and that it is her ring he took by force and gave to his mistress, the courtesan Bacchis. He then departs for Imbros without consummating the marriage. She is pregnant; her mother pretends she is ill and takes her home in order to conceal this from her mother-in-law. Pamphilus returns to find a baby born and keeps the secret, but refuses to take back his wife. His father accuses him of continuing his affair with Bacchis, but she refutes the charge. Meanwhile the girl's mother, Myrrina, happens to recognize the ring. Pamphilus then takes back his wife with their son.

AUTHOR'S PROLOGUE TO
THE MOTHER-IN-LAW
(2nd Production)

The title of this play is *The Mother-in-Law*. When it was first produced, it suffered from a novel form of interruption; it could neither be seen nor heard through the stupidity of the public whose interest was taken up by a tight-rope walker. Today it is presented as a new play. The author preferred not to repeat the former production so that he could ask for a fresh offer. You have known other plays by him, so please hear this one.

PROLOGUE TO THE THIRD PRODUCTION

(*Spoken by Lucius Ambivius Turpio*)[1]

In the guise of a prologue I stand before you to plead my case. Let me prevail on you to allow me in my old age to enjoy the just treatment I received in my youth; then I always managed to ensure the survival of plays whose novelty first brought them failure, and stopped an author's work from dying with him. When I first played in new plays by Caecilius, I was sometimes hissed off the stage and sometimes I just managed to hold my ground. I realized the hazards of an actor's career and decided to set my hopes and fears a definite task. I began to repeat the same plays, as a way of introducing new ones by the same author, always with the aim of not discouraging his efforts. I succeeded in putting these on the stage; once they were known they were a success. So I restored the author to his proper position, after the ill-will of his enemies had almost driven him from his love of his profession and the whole art of drama. But if I had poured scorn on his new works and set out to discourage him, so that his activity dwindled to nothing, I could easily have deterred him from writing any new plays.

Now give a fair hearing to my present case. Once more I am presenting *The Mother-in-Law*, a play for which I have never been able to gain a hearing before, so much has misfortune dogged its progress. You can remedy this by your understanding, if you will support our efforts. At the first production, the fame of some boxers, as well as the rumour that a tight-rope walker would appear, the mob of their supporters, shouting and women's screaming forced me off the stage

1. The actor–producer of Terence's plays.

before the end. I then decided to follow my old practice with this new play, to prove its worth. I put it on a second time. The first part was doing well when news arrived that there was to be a gladiators' show. Off rushed my audience, pushing, shouting, jostling for a place, leaving me powerless to hold my own.

Today there is no distraction, all is calm and peaceful: this is my chance to present the play and your opportunity to do honour to the stage. Do not be responsible for allowing the art of drama to sink into the hands of a few: make sure that your influence aids and supports my own. If I have never been greedy for gain in my profession, and have always held that my highest reward was to be wholly at your service, grant my plea on behalf of the author, whose interests are entrusted to my protection and your own sense of honour. Do not let him be the butt of unjust derision at the hands of unjust men. Let me persuade you to give his case a hearing, and then listen in silence. Others will then feel encouraged to write, and I shall be enabled to present the new plays bought at my own expense.

CHARACTERS

LACHES ⎫
PHIDIPPUS ⎭ *elderly neighbours in Athens*

SOSTRATA · *wife of Laches*

MYRRINA *wife of Phidippus*

PAMPHILUS *son of Laches and Sostrata, married to Philumena, daughter of Phidippus and Myrrina*

SYRA *an old bawd*

PHILOTIS *a young prostitute*

BACCHIS *a courtesan, lately mistress of Pamphilus*

PARMENO *Laches' elderly house-slave*

SOSIA *slave of Laches*

Two other slaves

A nurse

        (*Philumena does not appear*)

               ★

The scene is laid in Athens in front of the houses of Laches and Phidippus. To the audience's right the street leads to the centre of the town and the harbour, to the left to the country

[*The girl* PHILOTIS *and the elderly woman* SYRA *come on talking together.*]

PHILOTIS: Talking of lovers, Syra, precious few of them prove faithful to girls like me. Take Pamphilus for instance; he promised Bacchis no end of times that he'd never take a wife as long as she lived, swore it on oath so that anyone might have believed him. Now look at him – married.

SYRA: That's just why I'm always telling you not to be soft-hearted with anyone. You mark my words, catch whom you can, then rob him, fleece him, and skin him alive.

PHILOTIS: Can't there be exceptions?

SYRA: Certainly not. Nobody comes to you, you may be sure, who doesn't intend to wheedle you into letting him have his pleasure as cheaply as he can. You'd better see about setting your traps to get your own back, my girl.

PHILOTIS: All the same, it seems wrong to treat all men alike.

SYRA: Wrong to get your own back on your enemies? Wrong to trip them up like they'd trip you? Good lord, I wish I were your age and had your looks, or else you had my sense.

[PARMENO, *an elderly slave, comes out of* LACHES' *house talking to someone inside.*]

PARMENO: If the old man asks for me, say I've just gone down to the harbour to find out when Pamphilus is ex-pected. Are you listening, Scirtus? Only if he *asks*, mind; if he doesn't ask, say nothing, and the excuse can keep for another time. Why, here's Philotis! Where've you sprung from? How are you, my dear?

PHILOTIS: How are you, Parmeno?

SYRA: Good morning, Parmeno.

PARMENO: Good morning to you, Syra. [*Gallantly*] Well, well, Philotis, where have you been having fun all this time?

PHILOTIS: Having fun? Far from it! A brute of a soldier took me off to Corinth, and there I've had two years' continuous hell.

PARMENO: I'm sure you missed Athens, my pet, and cursed the day you thought of leaving us!

PHILOTIS: I've been longing to come back, I can't tell you how much, dying to get away from *him* and see you all again, and be with you all free and easy like we always were. There I couldn't say a word without being told first what *he* wanted.

PARMENO: I should like to see the soldier who could stop *you* talking, my dear.

PHILOTIS: I've been to see Bacchis – what's all this she told me? I could never have believed your master would take it into his head to marry while she was alive.

PARMENO: Marry, did you say?

PHILOTIS: Well, isn't he married?

PARMENO: I suppose he is, but it's a broken-down sort of marriage, if you ask me.

PHILOTIS: I hope to God it is, if that will help Bacchis. But tell me why I'm to believe that.

PARMENO: It's not a story to spread around, so you needn't ask.

PHILOTIS: I suppose you want to keep it quiet, but I swear to heaven I'm not asking you because I want to spread it around – I only want to enjoy it myself. I shan't say a word.

PARMENO: Clever, aren't you. But you won't catch me risking my skin on *your* word of honour.

PHILOTIS: Come off it, Parmeno. You know you're as keen to tell me as I am to hear – and more so.

PARMENO [*aside*]: She's got me there. It's my worst fault. [*Aloud*] If you promise not to breathe a word, I'll tell you.

PHILOTIS: That's more like you! I promise: go on.

PARMENO: Listen.

PHILOTIS: I *am* listening.

PARMENO: Pamphilus was just as much in love with Bacchis as ever when his father began to beg him to take a wife. The old man used the same arguments as all fathers do – he was getting on, he only had one son, and he wanted security for his old age. The boy refused flat at first, but when his father pressed him still harder he began to waver between his duty to his parents and his love. In the end he got fed up with being pestered and let the old man have his way and fix up a marriage with the daughter of our next-door neighbour here. Pamphilus didn't really take it seriously till the actual day of the wedding when he saw all the preparations made and realized it couldn't be put off. When it came home to him at last, his misery would have won sympathy from Bacchis herself, had she been there. He would steal off by himself whenever he could, and talk to me alone. 'Parmeno, I'm lost!' he would cry; 'What have I done? It's terrible and all my own fault. . . . I can't bear it. Oh, Parmeno, I'm so miserable!'

PHILOTIS: Blast that interfering old fool Laches!

PARMENO: To cut it short, he married the girl and took her home, but he never touched her that night nor the night after.

PHILOTIS: You aren't telling me that a young man could spend a night with a girl after a few drinks and keep off her? A likely story! I don't believe it.

PARMENO: I don't suppose you do, seeing that it's only desire that brings men to you; but this was an unwilling bridegroom.

PHILOTIS: Well, what happened next?

PARMENO: A few days later Pamphilus took me out of the house and told me that the girl was still a virgin and that before he married her he was hopeful that he could become reconciled to the marriage. 'But now I've realized that I just can't live with her any longer, it seems neither honest on my part nor good for the girl to carry on with this farce. I must return her to her parents in the state I received her.'

PHILOTIS: He sounds a decent fellow with the right sort of ideas.

PARMENO: 'On the other hand it won't do me any good to publish the facts,' he said; 'it would only be an insult to return a bride to her father when there's nothing against her. What I'm hoping is that when she finds I'm impossible to live with she'll end by going away herself.'

PHILOTIS: Meanwhile what about Bacchis? Did he go on seeing her?

PARMENO: Every day. But naturally when she saw he was no longer all her own she became thoroughly contrary and grudging of her favours.

PHILOTIS: Not surprising.

PARMENO: But what really broke things up was when Pamphilus began to have a better understanding of himself, Bacchis, and the wife he had at home, and started to think about the two women and the example they set him. His wife was modest and retiring, as a lady ought to be; she bore with all her husband's unkindness and unfair treatment, and said nothing of his insults. Gradually he came to think more of her, partly through pity and partly because Bacchis' indifference wore him down, until he drifted from her and transferred his love to the one whose disposition he found more like his own. Meanwhile an elderly relative died in Imbros, leaving the family his legal heirs. Pamphilus was packed off there by his father, protesting and in love, and left his wife here with his mother, Sostrata. His old father has buried himself in the country and rarely comes to town.

PHILOTIS [*bored*]: Are we ever coming to the breakdown of this marriage?

PARMENO: I'm coming to it now. For the first few days the women got on well enough together, but all the time the girl was developing an extraordinary dislike for her mother-in-law, not that there was any quarrelling or complaint from either of them.

PHILOTIS: What then?

PARMENO: If Sostrata ever came to her for a chat, she'd disappear at once and refuse to see her, and in the end when she couldn't stand it any longer, she pretended her own mother wanted her for some family ceremony and went off. She stayed away several days and then Sostrata sent for her, but she made some excuse. Sostrata sent again; no one brought her back. After repeated summons, the excuse came that she was ill. Thereupon my mistress went to visit her and was refused admittance. When the master heard of it he came back from the country, yesterday that was, and met Philumena's father at once. I haven't heard yet what passed between them, but I can't wait to know how it will all end. That's all. I'll be on my way.

PHILOTIS: Me too; I've got a date booked with a friend from abroad.

PARMENO: Good luck to you then.

PHILOTIS: Bye-bye, Parmeno.

PARMENO: Good-bye to you, my dear.

[*He goes off to the right and* SYRA *and she go off in the other direction. Almost immediately* LACHES *bursts out of his house in a fury, followed by* SOSTRATA *in tears.*]

LACHES: Ye gods, what a tribe they are! In league the lot of
them. Every blessed woman with the same likes and dis-
likes as all the others, and not a single one can you find
who'll show up a different mentality from the rest!
Mothers-in-law and daughters-in-law, they're all of one
mind – in hating each other. And they're all of a piece, too,
in setting themselves against their men-folk, the same
damned obstinacy in every one. I'd say they'd all learned
their cussedness at the same school, and if there *is* such a
school I can tell you who's head-mistress: my wife.

SOSTRATA: Oh dear, what have I done now? I can't
think.

LACHES: Can't you?

SOSTRATA: I can't, Laches, heaven help me and spare us to
live together in peace.

LACHES: Heaven forbid!

SOSTRATA: Some day you'll find how unjustly I'm accused.

LACHES: Unjustly? You? Is there any word to fit your conduct? You're bringing disgrace on yourself and me and the
family, and grief to your son in making enemies out of his
new relatives who were our friends and had thought our
son was a fit person to receive their daughter. You stand
out as a trouble-maker, you and your shameless behaviour!

SOSTRATA: *I?*

LACHES: Yes, you, woman. Do you suppose I've no feelings?
Am I flesh and blood? Because I'm mostly at the farm, do
you women think I don't know how each one of you is
spending her time? I'm much more alive to the goings-on
here than to what happens where I usually am, and shall I
tell you why? My reputation abroad depends on how you
behave at home. I heard long ago that Philumena had taken
a dislike to you, and no wonder; I'd have wondered if she
hadn't. But I didn't believe she could extend her dislike to

the whole household – if I'd known that, she should have stayed here, and you could have taken yourself off. [*Softening a little*] Sostrata, can't you see how little I deserve this distress you cause me? I went to live at the farm and look after our affairs out of consideration for you, so that our income could meet the expenses of a comfortable life in town for you and the boy; I'm always working, harder than is right and proper for my age. In return, you might have tried to save me from worry.

SOSTRATA [*sobbing*]: It's not my doing, it's not my fault this has happened.

LACHES: But it *must* be, Sostrata; you were here alone, and it can only be all your fault. I took over all the other responsibilities, and you should be responsible for things here. A woman of your age ought to be ashamed of starting a quarrel with a girl! Or will you say it was her fault?

SOSTRATA: No, Laches, I don't say that.

LACHES: Thank heaven for that, for my son's sake. I fancy *you*'ve no reputation to lose whatever you do.

SOSTRATA: How do you know she didn't pretend to dislike me so that she could be more with her mother?

LACHES: Nonsense; surely it's proof enough that when you wanted to see her yesterday no one would let you in.

SOSTRATA: Not necessarily. They said at the time she was very tired, and that was why I couldn't come in.

LACHES: It was something in *you* which made her ill, nothing else I'm sure, and no wonder; all you women want your sons to marry, and only the matches you fancy are arranged; then when you've pushed them into marriage it's you who push them out again.

[PHIDIPPUS *comes out of his house speaking to* PHILUMENA *indoors.*]

PHIDIPPUS: I know I have the right to compel you to obey
my orders, Philumena, but I'm too soft-hearted a father. . .
All right, have it your own way.

LACHES [*aside*]: Good, I wanted to see Phidippus. Now I'l
learn the truth. [*Stiffly, as* PHIDIPPUS *comes forward*] Phidippus, I know I may be indulgent to an extreme toward
all the members of my family, but not to the extent of
allowing my good nature to ruin their character. If you
were to follow my example, it would be in your own
interests as well as in mine. As things are, I see your women
have you under their thumb.

PHIDIPPUS [*indignantly*]: Indeed!

LACHES: Yesterday I called on you for information about
your daughter: you sent me away no wiser than I came.
If you wish this connexion between our families to continue, it is most unbecoming conduct on your part to leave
your resentment unexplained. If there has been any fault on
our side, kindly name it; we can then disprove it or make
such amends as you think suitable. But if your reason for
detaining your daughter is that she is ill, and you fear she
will not be sufficiently well cared for in my house, I take it
as a personal insult. Heaven be my witness, I cannot allow
that you care more for her welfare, though you are her
father, than I do myself; I do so on my son's behalf, knowing as I do that he values her more highly than his own life.
I am only too well aware how seriously he will view this
if he comes to hear of it; that is why I am anxious for her
to come back to us before he returns home.

PHIDIPPUS: Laches, I know the care and kindness to be found
in your home, and I am ready to believe that everything
you say is as you say. Please believe me now when I say
that I am anxious for her to return to you if I can prevail on
her in any way.

ACHES: What is stopping you? You don't mean she has anything against her husband?

HIDIPPUS: No, no. When I pressed her and tried to compel her to return she swore on oath she could not endure living in your home without Pamphilus. I suppose we all have our own faults, and I know I've always been a mild sort of man and simply can't set myself against my family.

ACHES: Well, Sostrata?

OSTRATA [*with renewed tears*]: Oh I'm so unhappy!

ACHES [*to* PHIDIPPUS]: That's definite on your side?

HIDIPPUS: For the moment it looks as if it is. And now, if you'll excuse me, I have business in town.

ACHES: I'll go with you.

[*They go off right together.*]

OSTRATA: There's no justice in the way our men blame all women alike, simply on account of a few wives whose behaviour brings disgrace on us all. I swear to heaven I'm innocent of what my husband accuses me – but it's no easy matter to clear myself when they've got it into their heads that all mothers-in-law are unkind. I *know* I'm not: I've always treated the girl as my own daughter, and I just can't think how this could have happened to me. All I can do is wait and hope for my son's return.

[*She goes back into her house. After a pause* PAMPHILUS *comes on right, from the town, talking to* PARMENO.]

AMPHILUS: Just my luck! All the hard knocks in love directed at poor me! To think how I've tried not to throw away my life! And I was so keen to be home again – only to find this! Damn it all, I'd rather live in any hole than come here and find things in this wretched state. If there's trouble ahead, the best thing for any of us is to gain what time we can.

ARMENO: Maybe; but this way you're more likely to find a

quick way out of your troubles. If you hadn't come, thi
quarrel would have gone on and on; as it is, I fancy you
arrival will pull them up short. You can learn the facts
settle their differences, and restore good humour all round
You're making far too much of trifles.

PAMPHILUS [*gloomily*]: You needn't try cheering me up. I tel
you I always had wretched luck. Before I married I wa
involved in another affair, but I never dared refuse the
wife my father thrust on me. Anyone can see without being
told what a rotten situation *that* was for me. I had scarcely
freed myself from this entanglement – and I'd just begun to
transfer my affections to my wife – when something else
happened to take me away from *her*. Now I find a situation
where I suppose either my mother or my wife's to blame
and isn't that just my luck too? I ought to bear with my
mother's faults as her son, but then I owe something to my
wife; she's been patient with me from the beginning and
never breathed a word anywhere about all she had to put up
with. But whatever happened, Parmeno, it must have been
something serious to set off a quarrel between them which
has lasted so long.

PARMENO: Nonsense, it's nothing. If you'll only use your
brains you'll see that it's not the worst wrongs which provoke the worst anger; for it often happens that one man
may find nothing to irritate him in a situation which would
turn a more irascible type into your worst enemy. Children
lose their tempers over little things simply because they
have so little self-control, and these women are like children
– no sound sense at all. It may have taken no more than a
word to start this quarrel.

PAMPHILUS: Go in then, Parmeno, and tell them I'm here.

[*Noises inside* PHIDIPPUS' *house.*]

PARMENO: What on earth's that?

PAMPHILUS: Shh. . . . I can hear hurrying and running to and fro.

PARMENO: Just let me get nearer the door. Did you hear that?

PAMPHILUS: Shut up. God, I heard a scream.

PARMENO: Shut up yourself, if I must.

MYRRINA [*inside*]: Hush, please hush, my dear.

PAMPHILUS: That sounded like Philumena's mother. Oh, this is too much!

PARMENO: Why?

PAMPHILUS: I can't bear it!

PARMENO: Can't bear what?

PAMPHILUS: I'm sure it's something awful which they're keeping from me.

PARMENO: They did say something about your wife having fits. . . . It might be that. I don't know.

PAMPHILUS: No, no, not that! why didn't you tell me?

PARMENO [*sulkily*]: I can't be telling everything at once.

PAMPHILUS: What's wrong with her?

PARMENO: Don't know.

PAMPHILUS: Hasn't anyone called in a doctor?

PARMENO: Don't know.

PAMPHILUS: I'm going in at once to know the truth. Philumena, my darling, how shall I find you? If you're in danger, I can only die with you.

[*He hurries into the house.*]

PARMENO: No good now my following him in; they hate the whole lot of us I think – yesterday they refused to let my mistress in. If this is some serious illness (though I hope not for the young master's sake) they'll say one of Sostrata's servants has been in the house, and then they'll cook up a tale of something brought in to make the girl worse and endanger the health and life of the whole damn lot of them. Then more blame for my mistress and trouble for me.

[SOSTRATA *comes out of her house.*]

SOSTRATA: I'm so worried by the noises I keep hearing next
door – I can't help fearing Philumena's illness has taken a
turn for the worse. Gods of healing, I pray this may not
be. . . . Now I *must* see her.

PARMENO: Madam –

SOSTRATA: Who's that?

PARMENO: – You'll find the door slammed again.

SOSTRATA: Oh, Parmeno, is that you? This is terrible; what
can I do? Mayn't I visit my son's wife when she's lying ill
next door?

PARMENO: Better not – nor send round anyone else, I'd say.
Love in return for hatred is double stupidity: useless effort
on your part and a bore to the other. Besides, your son's
here and went in at once to find out what's up.

SOSTRATA: Did you say Pamphilus is back?

PARMENO: Yes.

SOSTRATA: Thank God for that! This puts heart in me and
takes a load off my mind.

PARMENO: And that's the real reason why I don't want you
to go in just now. If Philumena feels a little better, as soon
as they are alone together I'm sure she'll tell him the whole
story of what came between you and how this quarrel
started. But here he is coming out again – *and* looking
awful.

[PAMPHILUS *comes out of the house, obviously much shocked.*]

SOSTRATA: My son!

PAMPHILUS: Mother!

SOSTRATA: Oh, I'm glad to see you safely home. Is Philumena all right?

PAMPHILUS [*with difficulty*]: A bit better.

SOSTRATA: God help her. . . . But why are you in tears?
What has upset you so?

PAMPHILUS: It's all right, mother.

SOSTRATA: What was the noise? Please tell me; was it a sudden attack of pain?

PAMPHILUS: That's right.

SOSTRATA: What exactly is the matter with her?

PAMPHILUS: A fever.

SOSTRATA: The recurrent kind?

PAMPHILUS: So they say. Please go in, mother, I shan't be long following.

SOSTRATA: Very well. [*She goes in.*]

PAMPHILUS: Parmeno, run and meet the boys and help them with the luggage.

PARMENO: Don't they know their own way home?

PAMPHILUS [*at the end of his tether*]: Clear off!
  [PARMENO *goes off right.*]

PAMPHILUS: I don't know where to begin on all I've seen and heard – it's all so unexpected: where can I start? I had to get out of the house. . . . I'm just about dead. It seems only a minute since I hurried in full of fears, expecting to see my wife suffering from something quite different from what I found. Ah! [*he groans*] The maids saw me coming and all cried out for joy as I took them by surprise: 'He's come!' Next moment I saw their faces all change because I'd chanced to come at such a bad time. One of them hurried on ahead to say I was there, and I followed hard after, all eagerness to see my wife. I saw what was wrong with her the minute I was in her room – more's the pity – there wasn't time to cover it up and she was too far gone to control her cries. I took one look, shouted something at her for her wickedness, and fled in tears, shocked and stunned by the incredible truth. Her mother ran after me, caught me up at the door, and clung to my knees, weeping, poor soul. I was touched; the fact is, I think, all of us are proud or humble only as circumstances permit. Then she began to speak: 'Oh, Pamphilus, now you see why she left your house. She was assaulted before you married her – we don't know the brute's name. She took refuge here to hide the birth of the child from you and the neighbours.' The very thought of her words sets my tears flowing again. 'Whatever chance brought you here today,' she went on, 'in the name of Fortune we both beseech you, if the laws of god and man permit, to say nothing and keep her misfortune hidden from the world. Oh, Pamphilus, if you have ever known her love for you, she begs you now to grant her this favour in return; it will cost you nothing. As for taking her back, you must do what suits you best. No one but you knows that this baby isn't yours; at least I presume it can't be, for people are saying that it was two months before you consummated the marriage, and you have only been married seven months. Of course you know all that. What I'm hoping and trying to do now, if it's at all possible, is to keep the birth secret from her father and all the neighbours. If it can't be kept from them, I shall have to say the baby is a seven-months child. I don't believe anyone will suspect you are not its true father when there's no reason to doubt it. I shall expose the baby at once; then it shan't be any trouble to you, and you will have concealed the wrong done to my poor undeserving child.' Well, I gave my promise and I'm determined to keep my word. But to take her back! It's all wrong and I can't do it, however strong the pull of our growing companionship and love. . . . These tears spring at the thought of my life in future and my loneliness. . . . Ah, fickle fortune! But I ought to have learned from experience with my old love, which I had to stifle by force of will; now I must do the same again. . . Here's Parmeno with the boys. He must be kept out of this at all costs, for he's the only person I told that for the first weeks of marriage I never slept with my wife. If he hears her repeated cries he must guess she is in labour. I'll send him off somewhere until it's all over.

[*He moves back as* PARMENO *and* SOSIA *come on right with slaves carrying luggage.*]

PARMENO: You were saying it was an awful crossing?

SOSIA: Damn me if I can tell you in words just how awful it is on board ship.

PARMENO: Really?

SOSIA: You lucky devil, you don't know what you've escaped by sticking to dry land. Cut out all the other miseries and take this one – all the thirty days and more I was aboard never a day passed when I wasn't in terror of death. That's the sort of foul weather we were having.

PARMENO: Horrible!

SOSIA: Don't I know it. I'd have bloody well cleared off rather than come home if I'd known just *how* I was to come.

PARMENO: It never took much to make you threaten *that*, Sosia. But look, there's Pamphilus outside the house. Go in, all of you, while I see if he wants me. [*To* PAMPHILUS] Still standing around, Sir?

PAMPHILUS: I was waiting for you.

PARMENO: What for, Sir?

PAMPHILUS: Someone must run up to the acropolis.

PARMENO: Who must?

PAMPHILUS: You.

PARMENO: Up there? Why on earth?

PAMPHILUS: Find Callidemides, the man I stayed with on Myconos, who was on the ship with me.

PARMENO [*aside*]: That's the end! The man must have taken a vow that if he ever got home he'd burst my guts with running his errands.

PAMPHILUS: Hurry along now.

PARMENO: What am I to say to him? Or am I just to *find* him?

PAMPHILUS: You're to say I can't keep my engagement t[o] meet him today, so he needn't wait. Be quick.

PARMENO: But I don't know what the man looks like.

PAMPHILUS [*distractedly*]: You can't miss him; a big man, red face, curly hair, fat belly, green eyes – and a face like [a] corpse.

PARMENO: To hell with him! Suppose he doesn't turn up[?] Am I to hang around all day?

PAMPHILUS: Yes. Now *run*.

PARMENO [*sulkily*]: I can't run. I'm tired. [*He trails off.*]

PAMPHILUS: Now I'm rid of him, but what on earth am [I] to do? How to conceal this baby's birth I can't think, muc[h] as I'd like to do what Myrrina asked; I'm sorry for the poo[r] woman. I'll do what I can, short of disloyalty to my mother[,] for I think she must have first claim on me however much [I] love Philumena. [*He looks down the street.*] That looks lik[e] Phidippus and my father, and they're coming this way . . [.] and I still don't know what to say to them.

[PHIDIPPUS *and* LACHES *come back from the town.*]

LACHES: Do I understand you to say she was waiting for my son's return?

PHIDIPPUS: That's right.

LACHES: I'm told he is here now, so she can come back.

PAMPHILUS [*aside*]: Now what reason can I give my father for not taking her back?

LACHES: Who's that speaking?

PAMPHILUS [*aside*]: I've chosen my road; no turning back now.

LACHES: Why here he is!

PAMPHILUS [*coming forward*]: How are you, father?

ACHES: Welcome back, my son.

HIDIPPUS: It's good to have you back, Pamphilus, and best of all to see you safe and well.

AMPHILUS: Thank you, Sir.

ACHES: Have you just arrived?

AMPHILUS: Only a minute ago.

ACHES: Tell me, how much did our cousin Phania leave?

AMPHILUS: Well, he was obviously a man who thought a lot of his pleasures in life, and his type don't do much for their heirs. The best that can be said of their sort of life is 'a good one while it lasted'.

ACHES: So that sentiment is all you've brought back?

AMPHILUS: And the bit he did leave, which is your gain.

ACHES: Or rather my loss; for I'd rather have him alive and well.

AMPHILUS [aside]: No harm in wishing that when he can't come back to life again, but I fancy I know your real wishes.

ACHES: Yesterday Philumena's father sent for her. [Nudging him] Say you sent for her.

HIDIPPUS: Don't prod me. Yes, I did.

ACHES: Now he'll send her back to us.

HIDIPPUS: Of course.

AMPHILUS: I know the whole story. I was told as soon as I landed.

ACHES: Blast all mischief-makers who go out of their way to spread news like that!

AMPHILUS [full of injured dignity]: Phidippus, I am satisfied that I have always been careful not to deserve insult from your family, and if I wished to recount here and now my fidelity, affection, and sympathy towards your daughter, I could certainly do so, did I not prefer you to hear it from her own lips. The best way of restoring your confidence in my character is for my wife who wrongs me now to do me justice. Heaven is my witness that this separation has come about through no fault of mine. But evidently she thinks it beneath her dignity to give way to my mother and respect her ways with proper deference, and it appears impossible for good relations to be restored between them; so I must choose whether to be separated from my mother or my wife. My sense of duty bids me put the interests of my mother first.

LACHES: Pamphilus, I confess it is good to hear this from you, and to know how you value your mother above everything; but are you sure resentment against your wife is not driving you to take up a wrong attitude?

PAMPHILUS [with emotion]: What resentment could drive me to be unjust to her, father? She has never done anything I could dislike to me personally, and more often did all I could wish. I have nothing but love and praise for her; I can only wonder at her feeling against me, and I long for her return. But since fate has snatched her from me, I hope and pray that she will spend the rest of her life with a husband who will be more fortunate than I.

PHIDIPPUS: It is in your power to prevent this.

LACHES: Of course, if you had some sense! Have her back.

PAMPHILUS: No, father. I have made up my mind. I shall devote myself to my mother's happiness.

LACHES: Where are you going? Wait a minute, please, Where –

[PAMPHILUS goes into LACHES' house.]

PHIDIPPUS: How can he be so obstinate?

LACHES: Didn't I tell you he would be annoyed? That was why I begged you to return your daughter.

PHIDIPPUS [exasperated]: Frankly I never believed he could be so pig-headed. Now does he expect me to go down on my knees? If he wants to take his wife back he can have her; if he has other ideas he must return her dowry and clear off.

LACHES: Here's another unreasonable person losing his temper!

PHIDIPPUS [*shouting after* PAMPHILUS]: Coming back in this state, the stubborn fool!

LACHES: He's got good reason to be annoyed, but he'll get over it.

PHIDIPPUS: Just because you people have come into a bit of money you're getting above yourselves!

LACHES: Are you trying to quarrel with me too?

PHIDIPPUS: He can think it over and let me know before the end of the day whether he wants her or not. If he doesn't, someone else shall have her. [*He marches into his house.*]

LACHES: Phidippus, wait, one word – he's gone. I don't care, they can settle it themselves as they like. Neither of them pays any attention to me or takes any notice of what I say. I'll take this quarrel in to my wife – she's at the bottom of everything and I can vent my spleen on her.

[*He goes in, and soon after* MYRRINA *comes out of* PHIDIPPUS' *house.*]

MYRRINA: I'm distracted, I don't know which way to turn; whatever can I say to my husband? I'm sure he heard the baby cry – the way he dashed into our daughter's room without a word to me. Once he finds out, what reason can I give him for having kept it all secret? Heavens, I can't think. Now there's the door – it must be him coming out. I'm lost.

PHIDIPPUS [*hurrying out of the house*]: My wife ran out when she saw me going in to Philumena. There she is, I see her. Here, Myrrina! Myrrina, I'm speaking to you!

MYRRINA [*nervously*]: To me, dear husband?

PHIDIPPUS: Your husband, am I? I wasn't sure you credited me with human feelings at all. If you'd ever thought of me as a husband, or even as a human being, woman, you wouldn't have made a fool of me with behaviour like this.

MYRRINA: What have I done?

PHIDIPPUS: Can you ask? Our daughter has had a baby. Well, have you nothing to say? Who's the father?

MYRRINA: Is that a question for her father to ask? Gracious me, who on earth do you think but her own husband?

PHIDIPPUS: I suppose he must be; as her father I can hardly think otherwise. What I can't understand is why you should have been so anxious to conceal this from us all, especially when the birth was normal and at the right time. [*A sudden thought strikes him*] Good heavens, is it possible you would rather destroy the child? Can you be so perverse? Can you prefer the death of the baby which would strengthen the tie between the two households to seeing your daughter settled with a husband who may not have been your choice? And I had thought all this was *their* fault! I see now it is yours.

MYRRINA [*in tears*]: I'm so unhappy!

PHIDIPPUS: I wish to heaven I could be sure about this. But I've just remembered your words at the time we accepted him as a son-in-law; you said you didn't want your daughter married to a man who kept a mistress and spent his nights away from home.

MYRRINA [*aside*]: Better any reason for his suspicions than the true one!

PHIDIPPUS: I knew long before you did that he had a mistress, Myrrina, but I never considered it a vice in a young man: they all do it. The time will soon come when he will blame himself for it. But you have never changed the attitude you took up at first, in the hopes of getting your daughter away from him and breaking the agreement I made. To-day's events prove your intentions.

YRRINA [*stung*]: Do you really believe me so perverse? Should I really behave like this to my own daughter if this marriage were for the good of us all?

IIDIPPUS: And have you the foresight or judgement to know what will benefit us? Perhaps you heard someone say he had been seen going in and out of his mistress's house. What of it? If his visits were discreet and not too frequent, surely it would be more reasonable on our part to turn a blind eye to them, rather than to ferret out the facts and thereby set him against us. And in any case, if he could break off relations immediately with a woman he had known for so many years, I should think poorly of him as a man, and certainly doubt his constancy as a husband for my daughter.

YRRINA: For pity's sake stop! Let's have no more of the young man and my so-called misdeeds. You go and find him alone, ask him whether he wants his wife or not, if he says he does, give her back, and if he doesn't – then I think I've done the right thing for my own daughter.

IIDIPPUS: If the unwillingness *is* on his side and you realized this fault in him, Myrrina, I was there and should have been allowed to use my own judgement in this. What makes me angry is that you dared to carry out your scheme without instructions from me. I forbid you to move the baby anywhere out of the house. [*As he turns to go*] But I'm the bigger fool to expect her to obey my orders – I'll go in and tell the servants not to let it be taken out. [*He goes in.*]

YRRINA: Was ever woman more unfortunate? If he discovers the truth I can see how he'll take it, when a much smaller thing can make him lose his temper like this, and

how to make him change his mind I've no idea. It will
the last straw if he forces us to bring up a child who
father we don't know. The night Philumena was assault
it was too dark for her to recognize the man, and she fail
to seize anything of his so that he could be afterwar
identified, though in the struggle he went off with the rii
she was wearing. And if Pamphilus finds out that anoth
man's child is being brought up as his, I'm so afraid he
feel he can't keep our secret any longer. [*She goes in. Afte
short pause* SOSTRATA *and* PAMPHILUS *come out of* LACHI
house.]

SOSTRATA: I know very well that I'm under suspicion, ho
ever much you try to hide it, and you think your wife lo
us because of something in me. But God be my witness a
grant me my deserts! I swear I have never consciously do
anything to account for her dislike of me. But you, m
son, have given me proof of your love, though in the pas
never felt I needed proof: your father has just been in
tell me how you have put my interests before those of th
woman you love. That has decided me to make you d
return and assure you that in my heart a son's affection h
its proper reward. My dear Pamphilus, this plan will I
best for my reputation and for you two: I have decided
go away and live at the farm with your father. Thus I sh
rid you of my presence and remove any reason whic
remains to prevent Philumena's returning to you.

PAMPHILUS: What on earth put that idea into your head?
her stupidity to drive you from town to bury yourself
the country? Certainly not. Besides, I'm not having ai
silly scandal-monger suggesting you went because of m
obstinacy and not through your own unselfishness. I've n
the slightest intention of letting you give up your frien
and family and the festivities you enjoy, all because of m

OSTRATA: But I don't really get much pleasure out of the things you mean. I had plenty of them when I was younger, and by now I'm tired of them. My chief concern is not to be a nuisance in my old age and not to feel people are waiting for my death. I can see that I'm disliked here, through no fault of mine, so it's time for me to go. I'm sure it's the best way to cut short all this argument on both sides, clear me of suspicion, and please our neighbours next door. Please let me be exempt from this universal slander of my sex.

AMPHILUS: With a mother like you I should count myself lucky in everything – if it weren't for my wife.

OSTRATA: Come, my boy, can't you make up your mind to put up with just one unpleasantness, whatever it is? If everything else is as you want it and as I take it to be, do this one thing for me: take her back.

AMPHILUS: I'm so unhappy, mother.

OSTRATA: So am I, my son. This distresses me as much as it does you.

[LACHES *has come out of the house during this and been standing unseen.*]

ACHES: My dear, I was standing within earshot and overheard your conversation. Now that is really sensible on your part, to adapt yourself to the changing needs of a situation and do now what you would only have to do later.

OSTRATA: I hope to heaven it is.

ACHES: Certainly you must come to the farm, and there I'll bear with you and you with me.

OSTRATA: I trust we shall.

ACHES: Go in then, and gather up the things you want to take with you; that's all.

OSTRATA: I will. [*She goes in.*]

PAMPHILUS: Father –

LACHES: What is it, Pamphilus?

PAMPHILUS: My mother shan't go away!

LACHES: What do you mean?

PAMPHILUS: I haven't made up my mind yet what to d
about my wife.

LACHES: What? What can you intend to do but take h
back?

PAMPHILUS [*aside*]: I do want her – I can scarcely hold myse
back – but I shall stick to my resolve. [*Aloud*] I must d
what's best, and I think the women are more likely to l
reconciled if I don't take her back.

LACHES: You can't tell; but in any case you needn't let
worry you once your mother has gone. Young folks nev
really like people of our age, and it's better for us to sli
away. You'll see us ending up like the old pair in the fairy
tale! But here's Phidippus, just when we want him. Con
and talk to him.

[PHIDIPPUS *comes out talking to* PHILUMENA *inside*.]

PHIDIPPUS: I'm angry with you too, Philumena, really ver
angry; you've behaved extremely badly, though I suppos
you have some excuse when you were put up to this b
your mother. There's no excuse for *her*.

LACHES: Ah, Phidippus, you've come at the right moment

PHIDIPPUS: What is it?

PAMPHILUS [*aside*]: What shall I say to keep this dark?

LACHES: Tell your daughter that Sostrata is leaving for th
country, so she needn't be afraid to return home.

PHIDIPPUS: But it's not your wife who's in any way to blam
for this, but mine; Myrrina was entirely responsible.

PAMPHILUS [*aside*]: The tables turned!

PHIDIPPUS: It was she who stirred up all this trouble betwee
us, Laches.

AMPHILUS [*aside*]: So long as I don't have to take her back, they can go on having all the trouble they like.

HIDIPPUS: For my part, Pamphilus, I should like our connexion to continue unbroken, if possible; but if you cannot feel the same, at least you must please take the child.

AMPHILUS: Damn it all, he's found out!

ACHES: Child? What child?

HIDIPPUS: We have a grandson, Laches. My daughter was expecting a baby when she was persuaded to leave your house, though I never knew of it until today.

ACHES: Bless me, that's good news! I'm delighted. A grandson, and the mother safe and well! But what sort of woman can your wife be? What a way to behave, keeping us all in the dark so long! Most improper – I'll leave it at that.

HIDIPPUS: I disapprove as much as you do, Laches.

AMPHILUS [*aside*]: Whatever doubts I had before I've none now, if she's presenting me with another man's child.

ACHES [*genuinely delighted*]: This should end all your indecision, Pamphilus!

AMPHILUS: Oh it's too much!

ACHES: This is the day we have often longed for, the day when you have a son to call you father. Thank God that day has come!

AMPHILUS [*groaning*]: I'm finished.

ACHES: Take back your wife, and no more argument.

AMPHILUS: Father, if she had really wanted to have children by me or to remain my wife, I feel positive she would not have kept from me what I now know she concealed. I can't help thinking that her feeling for me has changed; I don't believe we can ever live happily together after all this; so is there any reason why I should take her back?

ACHES: Your wife is young, and only did what her mother told her. There's nothing surprising about that. Do you

imagine you can find a woman who will be a perfect wife
What about husbands – haven't they their faults?

PHIDIPPUS: Settle it between yourselves, you two, whethe
you want to have her back or leave her with me. There'
be no difficulties on my side, either way: I can't answer fo
my wife. But what shall we do about the child?

LACHES: Need you ask? Whatever happens, of course yo
must hand it over to Pamphilus for us to bring up: it i
ours.

PAMPHILUS [aside]: Its own father hasn't taken much interes
– why should I bring it up?

LACHES [catching the last words]: What did you say, Pam
philus? Not bring it up? Are you suggesting we shoul
abandon it? You must be crazy. My God, I can't hold m
tongue any longer. You force me to speak of things I'
prefer left unsaid in the presence of your father-in-law
Do you imagine I don't know about your weeping an
whining and why you're in this state of distraction? Th
first excuse you gave for not taking your wife back wa
your mother; so she promised to leave home. Now you'v
lost that pretext, you've found another – you weren't in
formed of the birth of this child. If you think I can't se
what's in your mind you're much mistaken. Now please
at long last you can listen to me! How long did I give yo
to carry on an affair with a mistress? Did I ever grumble a
the bills I paid for what she cost you? I only begged an
prayed you to marry when it was high time you did, an
in the end I persuaded you. You did the right thing then i
complying with my wishes; but now you've gone back t
your mistress and she has put you up to this unjust treat
ment of your wife. I can see you've slipped back into you
old life.

PAMPHILUS: You think that of me?

LACHES: Yes I do. And I tell you it is an insult to your wife, trumping up false pretexts for breaking with her so that you can live with that woman with no one to witness your conduct. Yes, and your wife knew it. What other reason could there be for her leaving you?

PHIDIPPUS: Good guess-work. He must be right.

PAMPHILUS: I swear on oath that none of what you say is true.

LACHES: Then take back your wife, or give us a reason why you can't.

PAMPHILUS: It's the wrong moment –

LACHES: At least you can take the child: it is not to blame. I'll see about the mother later.

PAMPHILUS [*breaking away from them*]: Nothing can be worse than this; I'm at my wit's end. My father has me cornered at every point, damn it all! I'll go, I'm doing no good by staying here. I can't believe they'll acknowledge the child without my consent, especially as my mother-in-law will back me up. [*He slips away.*]

LACHES: Hi, are you running off without giving me a proper answer? Do you think he's in his right mind? We shall have to leave him. Give me the baby, Phidippus. I'll bring it up.

PHIDIPPUS: Thank you. No wonder my wife was in such a state; women are bitter about these things and find them hard to take. This was at the bottom of all the trouble, my wife told me so herself, but I didn't want to mention it while your son was here. As a matter of fact I didn't believe her myself at first, but now all is clear and I can see that he's temperamentally quite unsuited to married life.

LACHES: What do you think I should do, Phidippus? Have you any advice?

PHIDIPPUS: Let me see. . . . I think we should first approach this woman, and by questions and accusations or even a

pretty stiff threat try to find out if she has continued rela
tions with him since his marriage.

LACHES: I'll do that. [*He opens the door of his house and cal*
inside] Boy! Run over to our neighbour Bacchis and say
should like her to come here. [*The servant comes out an*
hurries off.] I hope you will stay and support me, Phidippus

PHIDIPPUS: Ah, Laches, I said before and I say again that
want the connexion between our families to continue, if i
is at all possible, and I hope it will be. But do you reall
want me to be present at this interview?

LACHES: Perhaps not, after all. You go and find a nurse fo
the baby.

[PHIDIPPUS *goes off and* LACHES *goes into his house. Afte*
an interval, BACCHIS *comes along the street right, accom*
panied by her maids. She is a woman of mature charm an
dignity, a complete contrast with PHILOTIS *in the firs*
scene.]

BACCHIS: There's some good reason why Laches asks me to
meet him, and unless I'm much mistaken I can guess wha
he wants.

LACHES [*coming out, in a great state of nerves*]: I must be carefu
to control myself or I shan't get as much out of her as
might. And I must do nothing I might afterwards regret
Now for it. . . . Good evening, Bacchis.

BACCHIS: Good evening, Laches.

LACHES [*increasingly nervous*]: I—I expect you must be wondering, Bacchis, why I sent the boy to fetch you here.

BACCHIS [*with composure*]: I'm a little nervous myself
Laches, when I think of my profession. I trust it doesn'
prejudice you against me; I can answer for my conduct.

LACHES: If that's so, you're in no danger from me, my goo
woman. I've reached the age when a lapse isn't so easily
forgiven, and I can't be too careful to watch my step. So

long as you intend to behave as an honest woman should, I would not dream of offering you a clumsy insult you have done nothing to deserve.

BACCHIS [*amused*]: Thank you, Laches. I can't be too grateful to you. I sometimes receive an apology *after* the sort of insult you refer to, but it doesn't help me much. And now, what can I do for you?

LACHES: You are in the habit of receiving my son Pamphilus.

[BACCHIS *makes a deprecating interruption*.]

LACHES: Please let me speak. Before he married I condoned this liaison – No, wait please. I haven't said yet what I meant to say. Now that my son has a wife, please find yourself a more permanent lover while you can pick and choose, for his feelings will not stay the same for ever, any more than your present age will remain unchanged.

BACCHIS: Who talks about a liaison?

LACHES: His mother-in-law.

BACCHIS: With me?

LACHES: Certainly: you. Moreover, she has removed her daughter, and because of this she planned to destroy secretly the child which has been born.

BACCHIS: I swear to you on oath, Laches, and I only wish I knew something stronger to make you believe me: I have had no relations with Pamphilus since the day he married.

LACHES [*after a pause*]: That is very good of you. . . . May I tell you, please, what I would like you to do now?

BACCHIS: What is it? Tell me.

LACHES: Go in to the women indoors and swear the same oath to them; satisfy their minds and clear yourself of this charge.

BACCHIS: Very well, though I doubt if any other woman of my profession would do the same, and show herself to a married woman for such a reason. But I don't want your son to rest under a false suspicion, and certainly you, as his parents, are the last people who should have the unjust idea that he's irresponsible. In fact, to do him justice, he should have all the help I can give him.

LACHES: Your words have won me over, Bacchis; I can truly say I wish you well. The women were not the only ones who thought this of him – I believed it too. . . . [*Stiffening again*] Now that I find you to be quite different from what I expected, I trust you will continue as you are, and then my friendship shall be at your disposal. Should you change – but no, I will say nothing you would not like to hear. I will only ask you to accept one piece of advice: try me, and what I can do for you, not as your enemy but as your friend.

[PHIDIPPUS *returns with the nurse who goes into his house.*]

PHIDIPPUS: I'll see you want for nothing in my house; there'll be plenty of everything you need, as long as when you've had all you can eat and drink you'll make sure my grandson is satisfied.

LACHES: Here comes our father-in-law with a nurse for the child. Phidippus, Bacchis has taken a solemn oath –

PHIDIPPUS: Is that her?

LACHES: Yes.

PHIDIPPUS: Her sort don't fear the gods, and I don't suppose the gods pay much regard to them.

BACCHIS: Take my servants – you have my leave to question them, under torture if you like. Our immediate concern is for me to make Pamphilus' wife return to him. If I am successful, I need not be ashamed when people say I was the only woman of my profession to do what the others avoid.

LACHES: Phidippus, we have proof that we wrongly suspected

our wives; now let us see if Bacchis can help. If your wife finds that her suspicions were groundless, she will cease to be angry with Pamphilus, and if he is angry only because his wife had a baby without telling him, why, that's nothing – he'll soon get over it. There is nothing at all here which could justify a divorce.

PHIDIPPUS: I only hope you're right.

LACHES: Ask Bacchis, she's here. She'll settle your doubts herself.

PHIDIPPUS: Why say all this to me? I told you before what *my* feelings were. It's the women you two must satisfy.

LACHES: Please, Bacchis, keep the promise you made me.

BACCHIS: You really want me to go in to them about this matter?

LACHES: Yes, please go; put their minds at rest and make them believe you.

BACCHIS: Very well, I'll go, though I know they'll hate the sight of me. Once a wife is put away by her husband she becomes the natural enemy of a woman like me.

LACHES: But they'll be friendly when they know why you have come.

PHIDIPPUS: I promise you they will be friendly when they have heard everything. And if you put an end to their mistakes you will clear yourself of suspicion.

BACCHIS: Oh, this is hard. . . . I'm ashamed to meet Philumena. [*To the maids*] Follow me in, you two. [*She goes into* PHIDIPPUS' *house.*]

LACHES: The best bit of luck I could ever hope for! Here's Bacchis doing me a service *and* making herself liked without it costing her a penny! If it's really true she has broken off relations with Pamphilus, she must know it'll bring her honour and glory and gratitude too; this good turn to him will make us all her friends.

[*He and* PHIDIPPUS *go into their houses. After a short pause* PARMENO *trudges on right, back from the town.*]

PARMENO: I wonder what the hell the master thinks I'm for, sending me off on a fool's errand like this. I've wasted a whole day hanging around the acropolis waiting for that fellow from Myconos. There I stuck all day like a prize fool, going up to every passer-by. 'Please, Sir, are you from Myconos?' 'No.' 'Then you aren't Callidemides?' 'No.' 'You haven't got a friend here called Pamphilus?' It was No all the time. I bet the man doesn't exist. I got fed up in the end, damn it, and cleared off. Why, there's Bacchis coming out of our in-laws'. What can she be doing there?

BACCHIS [*hurrying out*]: Parmeno, you're the very person I want. Quick, run and find Pamphilus.

PARMENO [*sulkily*]: What for?

BACCHIS: Tell him I want him here.

PARMENO: *You* do?

BACCHIS: No, no, it's for Philumena.

PARMENO: Hey, what's up?

BACCHIS: Nothing to do with you, so never mind.

PARMENO: Anything else I'm to say?

BACCHIS: Yes, tell him Myrrina has recognized the ring he once gave me. It's her daughter's.

PARMENO: I see. Is that all?

BACCHIS: That's all. He'll be here at once when you tell him. Only do stop dawdling!

PARMENO: I like that! What chance have I had of dawdling? I've done nothing but walk and run the whole blessed day. [*He goes off right.*]

BACCHIS: What happiness I have given Pamphilus by coming here today! I've brought him so many blessings and removed so many worries. I have saved his son, whom he nearly lost through his own fault and the women here;

I've given him back the wife with whom he believed he would never live again, and I've removed the suspicions of his father and Phidippus. And all this train of discovery was set off by a ring! I remember it must have been about nine months ago when he came running in to me soon after dark, alone, rather drunk, panting for breath, and clutching this ring. I was alarmed: 'Pamphilus, my darling,' I cried, 'how on earth have you got into this state? And where did you get that ring? You must tell me.' He pretended he hadn't heard me, but I soon saw through this and began to be still more suspicious; then I made him tell me. He confessed he had assaulted a girl in the street, he couldn't say who, and had pulled the ring off in the struggle. This is the ring Myrrina recognized on my finger. She asked where it came from and I told her the whole story; then it all came out that Philumena was the girl he attacked, and so her child is his own son. I'm glad he has found so much happiness through me, though I suppose other women of my sort wouldn't agree – it is really against our interests for a lover to be happily married, but all the same, I can't bring myself to play a mean trick for what I might make out of it. . . . So long as it could last, he was always a kind and generous and charming lover. His marriage hurt me, I don't deny, but thank God I can feel that I did nothing to deserve it. . . . Where men are concerned you must take the rough with the smooth.

[PARMENO *returns with* PAMPHILUS.]

PAMPHILUS: Are you absolutely certain, Parmeno, that what you say is really true? I don't want you to lead me on to a moment's false happiness.

PARMENO: I'm certain, Sir.

PAMPHILUS: Absolutely certain?

PARMENO: Absolutely, Sir.

PAMPHILUS: I'm in heaven if this is really true.

PARMENO: You'll find it true all right. [*He starts to move off.*]

PAMPHILUS: Just wait a minute please – I'm afraid I may have misunderstood you.

PARMENO: I'm waiting.

PAMPHILUS: I think you said that Myrrina has seen her ring on Bacchis' finger?

PARMENO: That's right.

PAMPHILUS: The ring which I once gave Bacchis? And it was Bacchis who told you to tell me – is that right?

PARMENO: Right again.

PAMPHILUS: Oh I'm the luckiest of men! There's no end to my happiness! Now what can I give you in return for this message? Tell me – I can't think.

PARMENO: *I* can.

PAMPHILUS: What then?

PARMENO: Nothing. I can't see what good you've got from the message, or from me either.

PAMPHILUS: You have restored me to life and rescued me from hell! Shall I let you go without a gift? You must think me very ungrateful! But look, there's Bacchis standing by our door, waiting for me, I think. I must speak to her.

[BACCHIS *comes forward to meet him.*]

BACCHIS: Well, Pamphilus!

PAMPHILUS [*eagerly*]: Oh, Bacchis, my own Bacchis, my saviour!

BACCHIS [*gently*]: It's all right; it was a pleasure.

PAMPHILUS: I shall have to believe you. . . . Oh, you still have all your old charm – it is always a joy to meet you, hear your voice, and see you come, wherever you are.

BACCHIS [*laughing*]: My dear, *you* are still your old self with the old ways. . . . There's not a man alive who can win hearts like you.

PAMPHILUS [*laughing nervously*]: Can you still say that to me?

BACCHIS [*suddenly serious*]: You did right, Pamphilus, to fall in love with your wife. I had never seen her to know her until today. She is what I would call a true lady.

PAMPHILUS: Do you mean that?

BACCHIS: I swear before heaven I do, my dear.

PAMPHILUS: Tell me, did you say anything about all this to my father?

BACCHIS: No.

PAMPHILUS: Then we needn't breathe a word. I'd rather this weren't like the comedies, where everyone ends by knowing everything. In our case, the ones who ought to know know already; and the others who don't need to be told shan't know a thing.

BACCHIS: Yes, and I can tell you something to make it easier for you to believe that the secret will be kept. Myrrina has told Phidippus that she believes what I said under oath; so she has forgiven you for everything.

PAMPHILUS: Perfect! And now I hope everything will go well for us all.

[PARMENO *attracts his attention so that he never notices that* BACCHIS *walks quietly off down the street, pausing to look back at him affectionately.*]

PARMENO: Please, Sir, can you tell me what exactly I'm supposed to have done for you today? And what you two were talking about?

PAMPHILUS: I can't tell you, Parmeno.

PARMENO: I might guess though. . . . But 'rescued you from hell' – how did I?

PAMPHILUS: You've no idea how much you've done for me today, and what misery you've saved me from.

PARMENO: Oh, but I *do* know, Sir, and I knew what I was doing.

PAMPHILUS [*humouring him*]: I'm sure you did.

PARMENO: Would I ever miss a chance of doing what was wanted?

PAMPHILUS: Come in with me now, Parmeno.

PARMENO: I'm coming, Sir. [*To the audience*] It seems I did more good today without knowing it than I've ever knowingly done before.

[*They go into* LACHES' *house.*]

The Brothers

[ADELPHOE]

INTRODUCTORY NOTE

The Brothers has always provoked discussion and is essentially a problem comedy, looking into the relations between fathers and sons, and setting out the conflict between the rival educational policies which in Rome were represented by the strict discipline of Cato versus the new liberal Hellenism. This is a question which every generation must try to answer – shall youth be guided by rules of conduct or allowed to have its fling? Both systems have had bad effects on the young brothers of the play: Aeschinus has been spoilt by Micio and is thoughtless and irresponsible, and Ctesipho lacks self-confidence and deceives his strict father Demea, though we feel Micio is right in insisting that they are both good at heart. Both the elder brothers are complex characters subtly drawn. For all his worldly wisdom, Micio worries about Aeschinus and has misgivings about having allowed him so much freedom; he pulls Aeschinus up sharply when the boy apparently intends to shirk the consequences of his folly. In the end Demea proves to him that a lot of his theorizing was no more than taking the line of least resistance. Demea is repressive and fussy, and at first may seem a conventional kill-joy until we realize that he has a sardonic sense of humour, and can thoroughly enjoy putting on an act to teach Micio a lesson. The sudden ironic end to the play has been variously assessed, but whether it is to be found in Menander's original or is Terence's own solution, it is surely not to be taken as a true change of heart on Demea's part – he may end more willing to allow some concessions to Ctesipho, but his principles are unshaken and he never does more than play a part. Micio does not seem so harshly treated if we remember that Pamphila's mother is not necessarily unattractive, and is certainly not likely to be the 'decrepit old hag' of Micio's exaggerated outburst. No doubt he will adapt himself to a different way of living with his usual ironic detachment.

The minor characters are well drawn – Hegio, the old family friend, Geta the excitable family retainer, and Syrus with his quick wits and ready tongue which recall Phormio in an earlier play. Syrus and his like were excluded from *The Mother-in-Law*, where Parmeno's part is cut to a minimum, and perhaps Terence brought them back into his last play to ensure its success with a popular audience. The episode with Sannio the pimp or slave-dealer, which Terence took from a different author, has been skilfully integrated into the play so that it provides much more than a comic scene. It serves to bring out Aeschinus' high-handedness in dealing with an inferior, and Ctesipho's nervous apprehensions about his father's knowing what he has been doing.

Terence provides no ready answer to the problems which engage him and which continue to be discussed today, and *The Brothers* is his last word before he met his unexplained end. It is a mature achievement and a unique contribution to classical literature.

PRODUCTION NOTICE

THE BROTHERS by Terence: performed at the funeral games for Lucius Aemilius Paulus held by Quintus Fabius Maximus and Publius Cornelius Africanus.[1]

Produced by Lucius Ambivius Turpio and Lucius Hatilius of Praeneste.

Music composed by Flaccus, slave of Claudius, for Sarranian pipes throughout.

Greek original by Menander.

The author's sixth play, written during the consulship of Marcus Cornelius Cethegus and Lucius Anicius Gallus.

---

1. The sons of Aemilius Paullus, both aediles in the year of his death (160 B.C.). The latter was already adopted into the Scipio family and is better known as Scipio Africanus Minor (See Introduction p. 9).

SYNOPSIS

Demea has two young sons. He gives Aeschinus to his brother
Micio for adoption and keeps Ctesipho. The latter falls in
love with a charming musician while under his stern
father's strict authority; his brother Aeschinus keeps the
secret, takes on himself the scandal and intrigue of the affair,
and ends by abducting the girl from a slave-dealer. Aeschinus
has also seduced an Athenian citizen, a girl in humble circumstances, and promised to make her his wife. Demea grumbles
and scolds; but soon the truth is revealed, Aeschinus marries
the girl he wronged, and Ctesipho is allowed to have his
music-girl.

AUTHOR'S PROLOGUE TO
THE BROTHERS

The author is well aware that his writing is scrutinized by unfair critics, and that his enemies are out to depreciate the play we are about to present; he therefore intends to state the charge against himself in person, and the audience shall judge whether his conduct deserves praise or blame. *Joined in Death* is a comedy by Diphilus: Plautus made a Latin play out of it with the same name. In the beginning of the Greek play there is a young man who abducts a girl from a slave-dealer. Plautus left out this incident altogether, so the present author took it for his *Brothers* and translated it word for word. This is the new play we are going to act; watch carefully and see if you think the scene is a plagiarism or the restoration of a passage which had been carelessly omitted.

As to the spiteful accusation that eminent persons assist the author and collaborate closely with him: his accusers may think it a grave charge, but he takes it as a high compliment if he can win the approval of men who themselves find favour with you all and with the general public, men whose services in peace, in war, and in your private affairs, are given at the right moment, without ostentation, to benefit each one of you.

After this, you must not expect an outline of the plot – the old men who come on first will explain part of it, and the rest will be clear during the action of the play. Make sure that your goodwill gives the author fresh enthusiasm for his work.

CHARACTERS

DEMEA ⎫ *elderly brothers. Micio lives in Athens and Demea*
MICIO ⎭ *farms just outside*

AESCHINU ⎫ *Demea's sons. Aeschinus has been adopted as his*
CTESIPHO ⎭ *son by Micio*

SYRUS   *a slave, Micio's head servant*

DROMO ⎫
        ⎬ *two of Micio's house slaves*
STEPHANIO ⎭

PARMENO   *Aeschinus' personal slave*

SOSTRATA   *a widow, Micio's next-door-neighbour*

PAMPHILA   *her daughter*

CANTHARA   *her old nurse*

GETA   *her slave and house servant*

HEGIO   *a neighbour and friend of her late husband*

SANNIO   *a pimp*

BACCHIS   *a music-girl*

*

*The scene is laid in Athens in front of the houses
of Micio and Sostrata. To the audience's right the
street leads to the centre of the town and the
harbour, to the left to the country*

[MICIO *comes out of his house calling to the servants within; as there is no answer he comes forward, and is revealed as a dapper middle-aged bachelor.*]

MICIO: Boy! . . . Then Aeschinus didn't come home last night from that dinner-party, nor any of the servants he took with him. It's true what they say: you may have stayed away from home or be late coming back, but you'll have a better reception from your wife for all her hard words and angry suspicions than you'll get from your well-meaning parents. Suppose you're late; your wife merely imagines you're involved in a love affair, or you are drinking and enjoying yourself and like to go off alone while she mopes by herself. Now look at me when my son hasn't returned, full of fancies and forebodings. The boy may have caught a chill or fallen down and broken a leg. . . . Why on earth should a man take it into his head to get himself something to be dearer to him than his own self? It's not as if he's my own son – he's my brother's, and my brother and I have had quite different tastes since boyhood. I've always chosen an easy life, stayed in town and enjoyed my leisure; and my married friends count me lucky never to have taken a wife. My brother's the opposite in every way – lived in the country, always saved, and chose the hard way; he married and had two sons, then I adopted the elder as a little boy, brought him up, and regarded him as my own. I've loved him like my own son: he has been my joy and sole delight. And I do all I can to ensure that he returns my affection. I give him money, turn a blind eye, don't feel called on to exercise my authority all the time; in fact, I've brought him up not to hide from me those youthful misdeeds which other sons conceal from their fathers. For a young man who has acquired the habit of telling lies and has the hardihood to deceive his father will find it all the easier to do this to everyone else. A gentleman's children should be treated honourably and like gentlemen. They can be restrained better that way, I believe, than through fear. But none of this suits my brother – he has different ideas. He keeps coming to me crying 'What are you doing, Micio? Why are you ruining our boy? Why do you let him drink and go after women, pay his bills for all this, and give him so much to spend on clothes? You've no sense.' Well, *he* has no feeling. It's beyond all right and reason, and it's utterly wrong (in my view, at any rate) to hold that there's more weight and stability in authority imposed by force than in one which rests on affection. This is the theory I have evolved; if the threat of punishment alone drives a man to do his duty, he'll be careful only so long as he thinks he may be detected: once he hopes not to be found out, he falls back into his old ways. But a man won by kindness is sincere in his behaviour, eager to make you a return, and doesn't change when you're out of sight. A father's duty then is to train his son to choose the right course of his own free will, not from fear of another; this marks the difference between a father and a tyrant in the home. If he fails to do this, he should admit he doesn't know how to manage his children. . . . But I do believe that's the man himself. . . . Yes it is, and I can see something has made him cross; I suppose I'm in for a scolding as usual. [DEMEA *comes on right from the town: shabby and workworn, he looks older than his years*.] Glad to see you well, Demea.

DEMEA: Good, I was looking for you.

MICIO: You look put out. Why?

DEMEA: Put out indeed! Can you ask me why, with a son like Aeschinus?

MICIO [*aside*]: I told you so. [*Aloud*] What has he done?

DEMEA: Done? He has neither shame nor scruple nor fear of the law! Never mind his past deeds; look at his latest!

MICIO: Well, what *is* it?

DEMEA: Breaking open a door, bursting into someone else's house, beating the master and the entire household pretty well to death, and making off with the girl he's carrying on with. The scandal's all over the town. I can't tell you, Micio, how many people came up to tell me; everyone's talking about it. Good heavens, if he needs an example, why on earth can't he look at his brother, thrifty, sober, living in the country, and managing his affairs in very different style? I'm talking of Aeschinus, but it's you I mean, Micio; you have let him go astray.

MICIO: Is anything as unjust as a narrow-minded man! He can only see right in what he has done himself.

DEMEA: What do you mean?

MICIO: Simply that you are all wrong, Demea. It is no crime, believe me, for a young man to enjoy wine and women; neither is it to break open a door. If you and I didn't do these things it was only because we hadn't the money. Are you claiming credit now for your youth restricted by poverty? How unfair! If we had had the means, we should have done the same. As for that boy of yours, if you had any humanity you would let him behave as a young man should, here and now; if not, he will only wait to bundle your corpse out of the house before carrying on just the same when he's past the right age.

DEMEA: Good heavens, man, you drive me mad! No crime for a young man —

MICIO: Now listen to me, instead of going on and on about

this. You gave me your son to adopt; he's my son now. If he does wrong, it's my affair, Demea; I meet most of the bills. He dines and wines and reeks of scent: I pay for it all. He keeps a mistress: I shall pay up as long as it suits me, and when it doesn't, maybe she will shut her door on him. He has broken a door-lock; I'll have it mended. He has torn someone's clothes; they can be repaired. Thank God I have the means to do so, and so far I haven't worried. Once and for all, either shut up or name anyone you like to judge between us; I'll prove it's you who are in the wrong.

DEMEA: Damn it all, why not learn how to be a father from us who really know!

MICIO: You may be his natural father, but morally he is my son.

DEMEA: You? A moral father?

MICIO: Oh, if you are going on, I'm off.

DEMEA: Leaving me like this?

MICIO: Why should I listen to the same tale again and again?

DEMEA [after a pause]: I'm worried, Micio.

MICIO: So am I, Demea, but we must stick to our own worries. You look after one boy and I the other. If you worry about both, it's as good as demanding back the son you gave me.

DEMEA: No, no, Micio.

MICIO: Well, that's how it seems to me.

DEMEA: All right, have it your own way. . . . Let him squander his money, ruin others and himself; it's no concern of mine. And if ever again a single word –

MICIO: Temper again, Demea?

DEMEA: Well, why not? But am I asking for him back? All the same, it's hard: he's my flesh and blood. . . . If I oppose – All right, I've done. You want me to look after one son, and so I do. Thank heaven he's a boy after my own heart.

The one you've got will learn some day – but I'll say no more.

[*He goes off right towards the town.*]

MICIO: There's something in what he says, but it's not the whole story. I don't really like it, but I wasn't going to show him I was upset. However much I try to placate the man, I only start arguing and put him off. He's being quite unreasonable, and if I were to add to his fury or even try to share it, I should soon be as crazy as he is. All the same, Aeschinus has treated me pretty badly over this. He has been the round of the whores, and they've all cost money; then only the other day he got sick of them, I suppose, and announced his intention of marrying. I hoped he was growing up and settling down, and I was delighted. Now it's all starting again! But in any case I must know the facts and find the boy if he's still in town.

[*He goes off towards the town.*]

[*The young man,* AESCHINUS, *comes on from the other direction with the music-girl,* BACCHIS, *and his slave,* PARMENO, *followed by the pimp,* SANNIO.]

SANNIO: Help, help, everyone, help a poor innocent man! I need help!

AESCHINUS [*to the girl*]: Don't worry, now just stand here. Don't look round, there's no danger, he shan't touch you while I'm here.

SANNIO: I'll have her in spite of all –

AESCHINUS: The scoundrel won't want to risk a second thrashing today.

SANNIO: Aeschinus, listen; you can't say you don't know my character. I'm a pimp –

AESCHINUS: I know.

SANNIO: – but as honest a man as ever was. You may apologize afterwards and say you meant me no harm, but I

shan't give that [*snapping fingers*] for it. Take it from me
I'll have my rights, and you'll pay with more than word
for what you've done to me. I know what you'll say: 'I'r
sorry, I'm willing to swear you were attacked withou
provocation.' Meanwhile the way I've been treated is
disgrace.

AESCHINUS [*to* PARMENO]: Go on, get a move on and ope
the door.

SANNIO: You aren't listening to what I say?

AESCHINUS [*to the girl*]: Quick, go inside.

SANNIO: No you don't!

AESCHINUS: Stand over him, Parmeno, you're too far off
here, close up to him; that's right. Now watch, don't take
your eyes off mine, and when I give the wink, be quick and
plant your fist straight in his jaw.

SANNIO: Just let him try!

AESCHINUS: Now look out! [*With a look at* PARMENO, *wh*
gives SANNIO *a violent blow*.] Let go that girl!

SANNIO: It's monstrous!

AESCHINUS: He'll give you another if you don't watch
out!

[*He does.*]

SANNIO: Oh, oh!

AESCHINUS: I didn't wink, but it's a fault on the right side
[*To the girl*] Now go in.

SANNIO: What's all this? Are you king here, Aeschinus?

AESCHINUS: If I were I'd see you got a reward of merit.

SANNIO: What do you want with me?

AESCHINUS: Nothing.

SANNIO: Do you know the sort of man I am?

AESCHINUS: I don't want to.

SANNIO: Have I ever touched anything of yours?

AESCHINUS: If you had, you'd suffer for it.

SANNIO: The girl's mine; I paid cash for her. What right have you to detain her? Answer me that.

AESCHINUS: You'd do better to stop this row outside my house. And if you go on making a nuisance of yourself, you'll find yourself *inside* being whipped within an inch of your life.

SANNIO: I'm a free man – you can't whip me.

AESCHINUS: Can't I?

SANNIO: You brute! Is this Athens where all free men are supposed to be equal?

AESCHINUS: If you've quite finished making a scene, you pimp, be so good as to listen to me.

SANNIO: Who's making a scene? I or you?

AESCHINUS: Drop it. Talk business.

SANNIO: What business? What talk?

AESCHINUS: Are you ready now to hear something to your advantage?

SANNIO: I'm all ears, as long as it's a fair deal.

AESCHINUS: Bah! Now a pimp wants me to stick to fair dealing!

SANNIO: I know I'm a pimp, the bane of youth, a plague and a liar, but I never did any harm to *you*.

AESCHINUS: No, that's the only thing to come.

SANNIO: Go back to where you began, please, Aeschinus.

AESCHINUS: You paid two thousand drachmas for that girl, and much good may it do you! I'll pay you the same.

SANNIO: What if I refuse to sell? Will you use force?

AESCHINUS: No, for –

SANNIO: Good; I was afraid you would.

AESCHINUS: The girl is free-born and shouldn't be sold at all. That's my view and I've laid hands on her to set her free. Now make up your mind, take the money or get up a case. You can be thinking it over till I come back: you pimp.

[*He goes into* MICIO'*s house.*]

SANNIO: Gods above, I don't wonder folk go mad with their injuries! That fellow has dragged me out of my house, beaten me, carried off my girl under my nose, rained blows galore on my wretched back, and on top of all he has done insists I hand her over at cost price. A nice way to behave, *and* he says he's demanding his rights! Well, I'm willing, as long as he pays up. But I know just what'll happen; once I agree to sell for a price he'll have witnesses on the spot to prove I *have* sold her. As for the money – moonshine. 'Soon,' he'll say: 'come back tomorrow.' I can put up with that too, so long as he pays up in the end, although it's a swindle. But I have to face facts: when you follow my profession you must put up with insults from these young men and keep your mouth shut. Well, nobody's going to pay me here. I'm only wasting time totting up accounts like this.

[SYRUS *comes out of* MICIO'S *house, talking to* AESCHINUS *within: he is a smart middle-aged manservant.*]

SYRUS: All right, Sir, I'll see the man myself. He'll be only too keen to take the money when I've dealt with him, and think himself well treated into the bargain. [*Coming forward*] What's this I hear, Sannio? Have you been having a scrap with my master?

SANNIO: Scrap? I never saw a fight on worse terms than the one we've just had. He dealt all the blows and I took them till we're both worn out.

SYRUS: It was your own fault.

SANNIO: What should I have done?

SYRUS: Humoured him: he's young.

SANNIO: What else did I do? I let him punch me on the jaw.

SYRUS: Come, you know what I mean. Forget money on occasion; that's sometimes the best way to make it. If you were afraid that if you gave in an inch and humoured the

young man that you wouldn't get your cash back – and
with interest – you really are a prize fool.

SANNIO [*sulkily*]: I don't pay down cash for expectations.

SYRUS: You'll never make your fortune, Sannio; you've no
idea how to set your traps.

SANNIO: Maybe your way's best, but I'm not sharp enough.
I've always liked to make what I could on the spot.

SYRUS: Go on, I know you. It's well worth two thousand
to you to keep on the right side of my young master; and
besides, I'm told you are off to Cyprus and [*ignoring
SANNIO's interruption*] you've made all your purchases to
take there and hired a boat. I know you can't give your
mind to this now, but once you're back again you'll fix
things up with him all right.

SANNIO: That's a lie! I'm staying here! [*Aside*] Damn it: that's
what set them on to this.

SYRUS [*aside*]: That stung him; he's afraid.

SANNIO [*aside*]: Curse him, look what a moment for a hold-
up! All those women and other things are bought ready to
take over to Cyprus. If I miss the market there, it's a hell
of a loss. If I drop this matter now and take it up when I'm
back again – no go, it'll have gone stale and all I'll get will
be 'Why come now? You raised no objection at the time.
Where have you been?' It would be better to cut my losses
than go on waiting here now or bring a case later on.

SYRUS: Have you finished working out what you stand to
gain?

SANNIO: Is this the right way for Aeschinus to behave? To
set about getting the girl back from me by force?

SYRUS [*aside*]: He's wavering: one word more. See if you
like this better, Sannio. Rather than risk saving or losing
the whole sum, halve it. He'll scrape up half the cash from
somewhere.

SANNIO: No, no! Now can't a poor man be sure of his capital? Has your master no shame? Thanks to him every tooth in my head is loose and my skull is one great bump with his blows. Now he wants to cheat me, does he? I'm not going.

SYRUS: As you please. Anything more, or can *I* go?

SANNIO: No, please listen, Syrus. Never mind how I've been treated, sooner than go to law just let me have back the money I paid for her. Up to now you've had no proof of my friendship, Syrus, but you'll see I'll be grateful and remember you.

SYRUS: I'll do my best. Look, here comes Ctesipho, all smiles about his mistress.

SANNIO: Now what about my request?

SYRUS: Wait a minute.

[*Enter* CTESIPHO *from the town, right, a volatile young man in high spirits.*]

CTESIPHO [*not seeing the others*]: Any man's welcome in time of need, but the real joy comes when your helper is the very man you want! Aeschinus, how can I find words to praise you? At least I'm sure that nothing I can say will be too good for you, and I know, too, that no one alive has what I possess – a brother who stands first in every virtue!

SYRUS: Sir –

CTESIPHO: Oh, Syrus, where is Aeschinus?

SYRUS: In there, at home, waiting for you.

CTESIPHO [*in raptures*]: Ah!

SYRUS: What do you mean by that?

CTESIPHO: What indeed! It's all his doing, Syrus, that I can live today! The splendid man! He put my interests before all his own, took on himself all the hard words and gossip, my own trouble and misdeeds; no one could do more. Who's that at the door?

SYRUS: Wait, it's your brother coming.

[AESCHINUS *comes out of the house.*]

AESCHINUS: Where's that dirty liar?

SANNIO [*aside*]: That's me, I suppose. Anything in his hand? Damn it, nothing.

AESCHINUS: Ah, good, I was looking for you, Ctesipho. How are you? Everything's settled now, so you can cheer up.

CTESIPHO: I can indeed, with a brother like you, Aeschinus, my own dear Aeschinus! I daren't praise you more to your face, or you might take it for flattery rather than true gratitude.

AESCHINUS: Oh, go on, you idiot, surely we know each other well enough by now. . . . I'm only sorry we heard of it so late – things had almost reached the point of making it impossible for anyone to help.

CTESIPHO: I was ashamed –

AESCHINUS: Not ashamed but stupid, to let a little thing like that nearly drive you out of the country. It's ridiculous. Perish the thought!

CTESIPHO: I'm sorry.

AESCHINUS [*to* SYRUS]: And now what has Sannio to say?

SYRUS: Oh, he's calmed down.

AESCHINUS: I'm going to town to settle up with him. You go in to her, Ctesipho.

SANNIO [*to* SYRUS]: Try now, Syrus. [CTESIPHO *goes in.*]

SYRUS [*to* AESCHINUS]: Let's go, Sir. This chap's in a hurry to be off to Cyprus.

SANNIO: Not so much hurry as you'd like! I've got time, and here I'll wait.

SYRUS: You'll be paid, don't worry.

SANNIO: But will he pay in full?

SYRUS: He will. Now shut up and come along.

SANNIO: I'm coming.

[AESCHINUS *and* SANNIO *go off right;* SYRUS *is following when* CTESIPHO *reappears.*]

CTESIPHO: Hi, Syrus!

SYRUS: What is it?

CTESIPHO: Do please pay that horrible man as soon as you can. If he carries on like this it may reach my father's ears, and that'll be the death of me.

SYRUS: I'll see it shan't. Now, courage, Sir; enjoy yourself with your lady indoors, and have dinner laid and all ready for us. I'll see this business settled and then come home with the fish.

CTESIPHO: Yes, do. Everything's so marvellous we must celebrate.

[*He goes back into* MICIO'S *house and* SYRUS *goes off after the others. After a short pause* SOSTRATA *comes out of her house, followed by the nurse,* CANTHARA.]

SOSTRATA: Please, nurse, how is my daughter? How is she getting on?

CANTHARA: She'll be all right, Ma'am, believe me. Poor dear, her pains are only just beginning. . . . You're not worrying already, as if you'd never seen a birth nor had a baby yourself?

SOSTRATA: Alas, I'm friendless here, we are two women alone – even Geta is out and I've no one to send for the midwife or to fetch Aeschinus.

CANTHARA: Bless you, he'll soon be here; he never lets a day pass without coming.

SOSTRATA: He's my sole comfort in my woes.

CANTHARA: And you couldn't have done better, Ma'am, as it turns out, once the damage was done, at least as regards him – such a nice young man, well-born and warm-hearted, coming from a grand home like his!

SOSTRATA: Yes, you're right; Heaven keep him for us.

> [SOSTRATA'S *elderly slave,* GETA, *rushes on right in a state of great agitation, without seeing the women.*]

GETA: Here's a state of affairs! O world, unite, take counsel, but what good will it do – such trouble as I'm in, and my mistress and her daughter too! O misery! Beset on all sides and no way out! Violence, destitution, injustice, desertion, disgrace! What times! What crimes! O wicked world, O vile wretch!

SOSTRATA: Heavens, why is Geta running about in such a state?

GETA: Honour, his promised word, pity, nothing could hold him back and turn him from his purpose – nor the thought that the poor girl he vilely seduced was just about to bear his child!

SOSTRATA: What *is* he saying? I still can't understand.

CANTHARA: Let's go nearer, Ma'am, please.

GETA [*dancing about*]: O woe! I'm nearly mad with fury. I'd like to see that household in front of me – I'd vent my rage on the lot while my blood is roused! I'd have vengeance enough if I could wreak it on them! First I'd choke the life out of that old villain who brought up this monster, then that Syrus who put him up to this, how I'd smash him up! I'd grab him by the waist and fling him up, I'd dash his head on the ground and spatter his brains in the street! I'd take that young man and gouge out his eyes and pitch him headlong! As for the rest of them, I'd rush and knock them out, hit and hammer and stamp them underfoot! . . . Now I'd best hurry and tell the mistress. [*He moves towards the house.*]

SOSTRATA: Let's call him. Geta!

GETA: Don't bother me, whoever you are.

SOSTRATA: It's me, Sostrata.

GETA: Where? I was looking for you.

SOSTRATA: And I was waiting for you. You're back in the nick of time.

GETA: Madam –

SOSTRATA: What is it? You're trembling.

GETA: Oh –

CANTHARA: What's the hurry, Geta? Get your breath back.

GETA: We are quite –

SOSTRATA: Quite what?

GETA: Done for. Ruined.

SOSTRATA: For heaven's sake, explain.

GETA: Now –

SOSTRATA: Now what, Geta?

GETA: Aeschinus –

SOSTRATA: What has he done?

GETA: He has abandoned us all.

SOSTRATA: No, it can't be. . . . But *why*?

GETA: He has found a new girl –

SOSTRATA: O heaven help me!

GETA: – And he makes no secret of it. He carried her off quite openly from the pimp.

SOSTRATA: Are you quite sure?

GETA: Quite, Madam. I saw it with my own eyes.

SOSTRATA: Oh no, no. What can one believe? Who can be trusted? Our Aeschinus, the life of us all, in whom we put all our hopes and everything, who swore he could not live a day without her! And he promised he would put the baby in its grandfather's arms and beg the old man's leave to marry her!

GETA: Madam, try to stop crying and think of the future; what ought we to do? Put up with it and say nothing, or tell someone?

CANTHARA: Heavens, man, are you crazy? Do you think this the sort of news to spread around?

GETA: No, I don't. First, the facts show he cares nothing for us. If we make this public now, he'll deny it, I'm sure, and we'll risk your reputation, Madam, and your daughter's life. And then, however much he might admit this is his doing, if he loves someone else it won't help your daughter to be married to him. So whichever way you look at it, best keep it quiet.

SOSTRATA [*after a pause for thought*]: No, not for the world! I won't.

GETA: What will you do then?

SOSTRATA: I'll tell everything.

CANTHARA: My dear Ma'am, think what you are doing.

SOSTRATA: Things couldn't be worse than they are now. In the first place she has no dowry, and then she's lost the next best thing – her reputation is ruined and she can't be married without one. There's just one thing we can do; if he denies it, I've got proof in the ring he sent her. Finally, my conscience is clear; no money, nothing unworthy of her or me has passed between us. I shall take him to court.

GETA [*dubiously*]: Very well, I suppose you're right.

SOSTRATA: Geta, you be off as fast as you can to our relative Hegio and tell him the whole story. He was my husband's dearest friend and has always looked after us.

GETA: Just as well, for no one else will. [*He goes off right.*]

SOSTRATA: You hurry too, Canthara, run and fetch the midwife; we must have her there when she's needed.

[CANTHARA *goes off to the town, right, and* SOSTRATA *into her house. After a short pause* DEMEA *comes back from the town.*]

DEMEA: I'm finished. Ctesipho, my own son, was with Aeschinus, they say, and had a hand in this abduction. This is the last straw, if the one who's still some good can be led astray by the other. Where am I to look for the boy? In some brothel I suppose, taken by that cad, you may be sure. [*Looking down the street, right.*] Now here comes Syrus: he'll know where he is, but he's one of the gang and if he guesses I'm trying to find him he'll never say a word, the brute! I'll keep it dark.

[SYRUS *comes back from the town with a basket of fish, pretending not to see* DEMEA.]

SYRUS [*aside*]: Well, we told the whole tale to our old man, just as it happened, and I never saw anyone better pleased.

DEMEA: Ye gods, the stupidity of the man!

SYRUS: He congratulated his son and thanked me for the advice I gave him. . . .

DEMEA: I shall explode!

SYRUS: He counted out the cash on the spot, and then gave me something to spend – which I've done to my liking [*looking in the basket*].

DEMEA: Here's the fellow for your orders if you want the job well done!

SYRUS: Why, Sir, I didn't see you. What's the matter?

DEMEA: Matter? I never cease to marvel at the way you people behave.

SYRUS: Silly I know, in fact to be honest it's ridiculous. [*Calls indoors as he hands in the basket*] Gut all these fish, Dromo, except that biggest conger. Let it swim in water for a bit and it can be filleted when I come back, not before.

DEMEA: It's a scandal!

SYRUS [*virtuously*]: I don't like it either, Sir, I often protest. [*Calls indoors*] This salt fish, Stephanio, see it's properly soaked.

DEMEA: Heavens above, does the man do it deliberately, and think he'll gain merit if he ruins my son? Damn it, I can

see the day when that young man will have to leave home
penniless and serve overseas.

SYRUS: Ah, Sir, you can look to the future as well as seeing
what's under your nose: that's true wisdom.

DEMEA: Tell me, is that girl still in your house?

SYRUS: She's there, indoors.

DEMEA: And she'll be kept there?

SYRUS: I suppose so; your son's crazy about her.

DEMEA: Impossible!

SYRUS: It's his father's foolish weakness, Sir. He spoils him
dreadfully.

DEMEA: I'm sick and tired of the man!

SYRUS: Ah, there's a world of difference between you and
him, Sir, and I don't say this just to your face. You're all
wisdom, from top to toe; he's nothing but notions. Now
you wouldn't have let your son carry on like this.

DEMEA: Of course not. I should have got wind of it at least
six months before it all began.

SYRUS: No need to tell *me*, Sir, how watchful you'd be.

DEMEA: So long as Ctesipho stays as he is, that's all I want.

SYRUS: That's right, Sir; like father, like son!

DEMEA: What about him? have you seen him today?

SYRUS: Ctesipho? [*Aside*] I'll pack this one off to the country.
[*Aloud*] He's been up at the farm for some time I believe.

DEMEA: Are you quite sure?

SYRUS: Oh yes, Sir, I went with him myself.

DEMEA: Splendid. I was afraid he was hanging around here.

SYRUS: And what a temper he was in!

DEMEA: What about?

SYRUS: Oh, he'd had a row in town with his brother over that
girl.

DEMEA: Really?

SYRUS: Yes, he spoke out all right. Just as the money was

being counted out, up he came unexpectedly: 'Oh, Aeschinus!' he cried, 'Fancy you doing this! Think of the disgrace to the family!'

DEMEA: I could weep for joy.

SYRUS: 'It's not just money you are wasting, it's your life.'

DEMEA: Bless him, he's a chip of the old block; I have hopes of him.

[SYRUS *shrugs his shoulders expressively*.]

DEMEA [*ignoring this*]: He's full of maxims like that.

SYRUS: Naturally; he could learn them all at home.

DEMEA: I spare no pains, let slip no chance, and give him a sound training; in fact I'm always telling him to look at other men's lives as in a mirror, and choose from them an example for himself. 'Do this' I say –

SYRUS: And quite right too.

DEMEA: 'Avoid that' –

SYRUS: Splendid.

DEMEA: 'This does you credit' –

SYRUS: That's the way.

DEMEA: 'There you'll be wrong' –

SYRUS: Perfect.

DEMEA: 'And then' –

SYRUS: Excuse me, Sir, I haven't time at the moment to listen to you. I've got just the fish I wanted and I must see they're not spoiled. It's as bad a fault in us servants not to see to such things as it is in you and yours, Sir, not to do what you've just been saying, and as far as I can I train the other servants on the same lines as you. 'This is too salt,' I say, 'this is burnt to a cinder, this is not cleaned properly; but that's just right, remember to do that next time.' I spare no pains to give all the advice I can, as I understand it, and I end up by telling them to look in the pans like a mirror, Sir, while I tell them what they ought to do. All this sounds silly I know, but what would you have us do? You have to take men as they are. . . . Anything else you want, Sir?

DEMEA [*angrily*]: Only that you had more sense.

SYRUS: You're off to the country now?

DEMEA: At once.

SYRUS [*blandly*]: Well, if no one takes your good advice, you're not really doing much good here, are you, Sir? [*He goes into* MICIO'S *house.*]

DEMEA: Off to the country then, as the boy I wanted here is there already. He belongs to me, and he's the one to worry about. As for the other one, Micio can see to him, as that's what he wants. Now who can I see coming? Hegio, I do believe, if my eyes don't deceive me, my old boyhood friend, a man of worth and honour of the good old sort, and heaven knows we need citizens like him! It will be a long day before the country suffers anything from *him*. This warms my heart; as long as I can set eyes on one of his kind, life's worth living. I'll wait here to greet him and have a word with him.

[GETA *returns right, talking to* HEGIO, *and not seeing* DEMEA.]

HEGIO: Good heavens, Geta, what a monstrous story. Can it be true?

GETA: It's a fact, Sir.

HEGIO: Such ungentlemanly conduct in a member of that family! Aeschinus, this is not like your father's son!

DEMEA [*aside*]: He must have heard about that girl. *He* can feel it, though it's not his son, while the boy's own father thinks nothing of it. Damn it, I wish Micio were here to listen to him!

HEGIO: They must do the right thing; they shan't get away with this.

GETA: We depend on you, Sir: you're all we have and w
all look to you as our father and protector. Our old maste
entrusted us to you with his dying words, and if yo
abandon us we're lost.

HEGIO: Never: don't talk like that. I can't do enough whe
duty calls me.

DEMEA: I'll meet him. [*Coming forward*] Hegio, I hope wit
all my heart I see you well.

HEGIO [*coldly*]: Oh, I was looking for you. The same to you
Demea.

DEMEA: You wanted me?

HEGIO: Yes. Your elder son Aeschinus, the one you gave to
your brother to adopt, has shown himself neither an hones
man nor a gentleman.

DEMEA: What do you mean?

HEGIO: You knew our old friend Simulus –

DEMEA: Of course I did.

HEGIO: Your son has seduced his daughter.

DEMEA: Oh no!

HEGIO: Wait, Demea; you haven't heard the worst.

DEMEA: Can anything be worse?

HEGIO: Yes indeed. This could have been borne somehow –
there were excuses: darkness, passion, drink, and youth; it
is human nature. When he realized what he had done, he
went of his own accord to the mother, weeping, begging,
praying, promising, and swearing to marry the girl. He was
forgiven and trusted, and the matter was hushed up. The
girl was pregnant, and today her time is near. Now our fine
gentleman has bought himself another girl to live with,
some sort of music girl, heaven help us, and the other is
abandoned.

DEMEA: Are you sure this is true?

HEGIO: The girl is here and her mother too, and the facts

are obvious; then there's Geta, an honest man as slaves go,
and an active one – he's the prop and mainstay of the whole
household. Take him, tie him up, get the truth out of him!

GETA: Put me on the rack, Sir, if that's not the truth. Besides, the boy won't deny it; bring him face to face with
me.

DEMEA [*aside*]: I'm ashamed. I can't think what to do or say
to him.

PAMPHILA [*from inside the house*]: Ah, the pain! Juno Lucina,
help me, save me, save me!

HEGIO: What, has her labour started?

GETA: It must have, Sir.

HEGIO: Now you can hear her calling on the honour of your
family, Demea. Do what you must do, and let it be of your
own good will. I pray heaven you will take the proper
course, but if your intentions are otherwise, I warn you I
shall defend this girl and her dead father with all my power.
He was my relative, and we were brought up together from
our earliest childhood; we stood together in peace and war,
and together we faced the hardships of poverty to the end.
Hence I shall make every effort, do all I can, go to law if
need be, lay down my life in fact, before I fail these women.
. . . What is your answer?

DEMEA [*at a loss*]: I'll find my brother, Hegio, and do
what he advises.

HEGIO: But bear this in mind, Demea. The more easy your
life, the higher you people rise in power, wealth, good
fortune, and rank, the more you must judge rightly what is
right and fair, if you want to be known as honest men.

DEMEA: You needn't stay; everything proper shall be done.

HEGIO: That is no more than your duty. Geta, take me in to
Sostrata.

[*They go into* SOSTRATA'S *house.*]

DEMEA: I warned him this would happen. I only hope it will end here! But indulgence carried so far is bound to end in disaster of some sort. I'll go and find my brother and pour out the whole story.

[*He goes off right.*]

HEGIO [*coming out of the house*]: Bear up, Sostrata, and do what you can to comfort her. I'll find Micio, if he's in town, and tell him exactly what has happened. If he intends to do his duty, I hope he will. But if he has other ideas, he must give me an answer so that I know at once what steps to take.

[*He goes off, right, towards the town. Almost immediately* CTESIPHO *and* SYRUS *come out of* MICIO'S *house.*]

CTESIPHO: Do you really mean my father has gone off to the country?

SYRUS: Yes, some time ago.

CTESIPHO: Go on, please, tell me all about it.

SYRUS: He's at the farm, busy with something at this very moment, I expect.

CTESIPHO: I hope he is! And so long as he doesn't kill himself, I wish he'd end up so tired that for the next three days he'd be unable to get out of bed!

SYRUS: Hear, hear; or something even better.

CTESIPHO: Agreed. All I want is to spend this whole day as happily as I began. There's only one thing I don't like about our farm – it's too near. If it were farther off he couldn't be back before dark. As it is, I know what'll happen: he won't find me there, so he'll come running back here to ask me where I've been. 'I haven't seen you all day.' What's the answer to that?

SYRUS: Can't you think of anything?

CTESIPHO: Nothing at all.

SYRUS: The more fool you. Haven't you a dependant, a companion, or a friend?

CTESIPHO: Of course I have. What then?

SYRUS: You could have been doing business with them.

CTESIPHO: But I wasn't. I can't say that.

SYRUS: Yes you can.

CTESIPHO [*dubiously*]: That might account for the day. . . . If I spend the night here, what excuse have I then?

SYRUS: Oh, if only people made a habit of doing business by night as well! Never mind, don't worry, I know him and his ways. Let him rage, and I'll soon have him as quiet as a lamb.

CTESIPHO: How?

SYRUS: He likes to hear the best of you. I can sing your praises to heaven and go through the list of all your virtues.

CTESIPHO: *My* virtues?

SYRUS: Yours all right. I can have the old man crying like a child for joy. Now look out!

CTESIPHO: What is it?

SYRUS: Talk of the devil. . . .

CTESIPHO: Is it my father?

SYRUS: His very self.

CTESIPHO: Oh, Syrus, what are we to do?

SYRUS: Quick, go in. I'll see to it.

CTESIPHO: If he wants me you haven't seen me, do you hear?

SYRUS: You be quiet!

[*He pushes* CTESIPHO *into the house and stands back, by the door.* DEMEA *returns from the town.*]

DEMEA: Just my luck! First I can't find my brother anywhere; then while I'm looking for him I run into one of the farm hands and he tells me Ctesipho is *not* at the farm. Now I don't know what to do.

CTESIPHO [*putting his head out*]: Syrus!

SYRUS: What?

CTESIPHO: Is it me he wants?

SYRUS: Yes.

CTESIPHO: Then I'm done for.

SYRUS: Bear up.

DEMEA [*still talking to himself*]: Nothing but bad luck ... wha
the devil does it mean? I can't make it out. Maybe I'm to
believe I was born for nothing but misery. I was the firs
to guess our troubles, the first to find everything out, the
first to give the bad news. Whatever happens, I'm the one
who suffers.

SYRUS [*aside*]: He makes me laugh. The first to know! He's
the only one who hasn't a clue.

DEMEA: Now I'm back to see if Micio's home again.

CTESIPHO [*peeping out*]: Syrus! For heaven's sake don't let
him in here.

SYRUS: Be quiet, can't you? I'm doing my best.

CTESIPHO: Yes, I dare say, but I just can't trust you. I'll
find a room and lock myself in with her, that'll be
safest.

SYRUS: All right. I'll move him on, anyway.

DEMEA: There's that scoundrel Syrus.

SYRUS [*aloud, pretending not to see* DEMEA]: How the devil
can anyone carry on here at this rate! I should just like to
know how many masters a poor chap's supposed to have.
It's a dog's life!

DEMEA: What's all this whining about? What can he want?
Now my man, is my brother at home?

SYRUS: Why the hell do you call me your man? I'm finished.

DEMEA: What's the matter with you?

SYRUS: Matter? Ctesipho's pretty well pummelled me to
death, and ill-treated that girl too.

DEMEA: What's that you say?

SYRUS: Just you take a look at the way he's split my lip.

DEMEA: Why was that?

SYRUS: He says it was all my doing when the girl was bought.

DEMEA: I thought you said just now that you'd gone with him to the farm.

SYRUS: We did go, but he came back in a towering rage. He spared nothing. Fancy not being ashamed to beat an old man like me! Why it seems only yesterday I held him in my arms and he was only *so* high.

DEMEA: Splendid! You're your father's son, Ctesipho, and the man for me!

SYRUS: Splendid indeed! If he's any sense he'll keep his fists to himself in future.

DEMEA: Well done!

SYRUS: Oh very, beating up a wretched girl and a poor slave who didn't dare hit back. Oh yes, well done!

DEMEA: Couldn't be better. He sees as I do that you're at the bottom of all this. Now, is my brother at home?

SYRUS [*sulkily*]: No he isn't.

DEMEA: I wonder where I can find him.

SYRUS: I know all right, but you can ask all day – I shan't tell you.

DEMEA: You say that?

SYRUS: Yes, I do.

DEMEA: Then I'll knock your head off here and now.

SYRUS: Well, there's a man. . . . I don't know his name, but I know where to find him.

DEMEA: Tell me then.

SYRUS: You know the colonnade near the meat market, down that way?

DEMEA: Of course I do.

SYRUS: Go straight up the street past it. Then there's a turning going downhill; go straight down and you'll see a chapel on this side and next to it that alley –

DEMEA: Which one?

SYRUS: Where there's a big fig tree.

DEMEA: I know.

SYRUS: Go on through it.

DEMEA [*after some thought*]: That alley hasn't *got* a wa
through.

SYRUS: So it hasn't. What a fool I am! My mistake. Go bac
to the colonnade. Yes, this is a much shorter way and les
chance of going wrong. Do you know Cratinus' house
that rich fellow's?

DEMEA: Yes.

SYRUS: Go past it, turn left, straight up the street, come to th
Temple of Diana, then turn right and before you come t
the town gate just by the pond there's a small flour mil
and a workshop opposite. . . . That's where he is.

DEMEA [*suspiciously*]: What's he doing there?

SYRUS [*airily*]: Oh, giving orders for some garden seats . .
to be made with oak legs.

DEMEA: For one of your drinking-parties I suppose. Very
nice too! I'll be off.

[*He goes off to the town, right.*]

SYRUS: That's right, go; and today I've given you the
marching orders you deserve, old drybones. Well, Aeschinus is horribly late, lunch is spoiling, and Ctesipho – all *he*
wants is love. That gives me time for myself. I'll go and
have a sip of the wine and a pick at all the best bits . . . a
nice easy way to spend a day like this.

[*He goes into the house.* MICIO *and* HEGIO *come on right
together from the town.*]

MICIO: I really can't see I deserve your praise for this, Hegio.
The offence was on our side, and it is no more than my
duty to put things right. I know there are men who see a
wanton insult in any criticism of their conduct and deli-

berately turn the attack on their critics, but did you expect this from me? Are you thanking me for being different?

HEGIO: No, no, of course not. I never thought you other than you are, Micio. But now please come with me to the girl's mother and tell her in person all you've said to me, that all her suspicions of Aeschinus were on account of his brother and that music-girl.

MICIO: I'm quite ready, if we must and you think it's the right thing.

HEGIO: That's good of you. She's wearing herself out with trouble and worry, and you can take this weight off her mind. It will be a duty well done. But if you prefer, I can tell her what you've said to me.

MICIO: No, I'll go.

HEGIO: It really is good of you. People who are not so lucky in life always tend to be a bit suspicious and ready to take offence at everything; I suppose their poverty makes them imagine slights. If you can explain to her yourself she'll take it better.

MICIO: True: how right you are.

HEGIO: Come in with me then.

MICIO: Certainly.

[*They go into* SOSTRATA'S *house; there is a short pause, then* AESCHINUS *hurries on right and paces about distractedly*.]

AESCHINUS: This is sheer torture! I never thought to receive such a frightful blow. I just can't think what I'm to do with myself or what to do at all. I'm numb with terror, dazed with fear, robbed of reasoning power! How can I find a way out of this mess? This awful suspicion – it seemed all too natural! Sostrata is convinced I bought this girl for myself – so I discovered from the old woman when I caught sight of her on her way to fetch the midwife; I ran up and asked her how Pamphila was, whether labour had

started and the midwife had been sent for. 'Get out!' was
all she said. 'Clear off, Aeschinus, we've had enough of your
lying words and your broken promises!' 'What on earth
do you mean by that?' I said. 'Good-bye, you can keep the
girl you've chosen.' I guessed at once what they suspected,
but held my tongue – one word about my brother to that
old gossip and all would be out.

Now what can I do? Say the girl is my brother's? But
this must be kept dark at all costs. I can't let it out if it's still
possible to keep the secret. . . . Besides, I doubt it they would
believe me: it all hangs together and sounds likely enough.
It was I who carried off the girl and I who paid the money,
and our house she was brought to. This at least was all my
doing, I admit. If only I had told the whole wretched story
to my father! If I'd asked him he'd have let me marry
Pamphila. . . . [*After a pause*] Here I am, still putting things
off! Now's the time, Aeschinus, to pull yourself together!
And first of all I'll go to the women and clear myself.
[*He moves towards* SOSTRATA'S *house.*] Here's the door. . . .
No, I can't face it. . . . I'm a coward, I can never raise a
hand to this door without a shudder. . . . [*He makes a
tremendous effort and knocks loudly*] Anyone there? It's
Aeschinus. Open the door, somebody, at once! Someone's
coming out; I'll stay here out of sight.

[MICIO *comes out of* SOSTRATA'S *house speaking back to
her.*]

MICIO: Do as I say, Sostrata, both of you, while I find
Aeschinus and tell him our arrangements. [*Coming forward*]
Someone knocked – who was it?

AESCHINUS [*aside*]: Heavens, it's my father; I'm done for!

MICIO: Aeschinus!

AESCHINUS [*aside*]: What can he want?

MICIO: Was it you who knocked? [*Aside*] No reply; I think

I must tease him a bit – he deserves it for never wanting to tell me anything. [*Aloud*] Can't you answer me?

AESCHINUS [*in confusion*]: I didn't knock – at least I don't think I did.

MICIO: No? I was just wondering what you were doing here. [*Aside*] He's blushing: all's well.

AESCHINUS: Excuse me, father, but what took you there? [*pointing to* SOSTRATA'S *house*].

MICIO: No business of mine. A friend brought me here just now to act as a witness.

AESCHINUS: Witness for what?

MICIO [*watching him closely*]: I'll tell you. There are some women living there, in a poor way. I don't think you know them, in fact I am sure you can't, for they have not been here long.

AESCHINUS: Well, what then?

MICIO: There is a girl with her mother –

AESCHINUS: Go on –

MICIO: The girl has lost her father, and this friend of mine is her next-of-kin; so he must marry her. That's the law.

AESCHINUS [*aside*]: No – I can't bear it.

MICIO: What was that?

AESCHINUS: Nothing: it's all right: go on.

MICIO: He has come to take her away to Miletus – where he lives.

AESCHINUS: What, to take the girl away?

MICIO: That's right.

AESCHINUS: All the way to Miletus did you say?

MICIO: I did.

AESCHINUS [*aside*]: Oh my heart will burst! [*Aloud*] But the women – what do they say?

MICIO: What do you expect? Some nonsense. The mother has a trumped-up story about the girl having a baby by another man, whom she won't name. He came first, she says, so the girl ought not to be married to my friend.

AESCHINUS: Then don't you think that's right?

MICIO: No, I don't.

AESCHINUS: You don't? And will he really take her away, father?

MICIO: Why on earth shouldn't he?

AESCHINUS [*in a passionate outburst*]: It was cruel of you both, it was monstrous, and if I must speak plainly, father, it was – it was – downright dishonourable!

MICIO: But *why*?

AESCHINUS: You ask me why? What about the unhappy man who first loved her and for all I know, poor wretch, still loves her desperately? What do you suppose *he* will feel when he sees her torn from his arms and carried off before his very eyes? I tell you, father, it's a sin and a scandal!

MICIO: How do you make that out? Who promised this girl in marriage and who gave her away? Who was the bridegroom and when was the wedding? Who witnessed it? She was meant for another – why did this man take her?

AESCHINUS: Then was this girl to sit at home, at her age, waiting for a relative to turn up from heaven knows where? You could have said *that*, father, and stuck to it.

MICIO: Nonsense! I came to help a friend; was I to turn against him? In any case, Aeschinus, the girl is no concern of ours. Why should we bother about them? Let us go. . . . But what's the matter? You are crying?

AESCHINUS: Father, please listen. . . .

MICIO [*gently*]: My son, I have heard the whole story; I understand, for I love you, so all you do touches my heart.

AESCHINUS: Then I'll try to deserve your love in future all your life, father – I feel so guilty and ashamed of what I've done, I can't look you in the face.

MICIO: I believe you; I know you are honourable at heart. But I worry about you and your heedless ways. What sort of a country do you think you live in? You seduced a girl you should never have touched. That was your first fault, and quite bad enough, though no more than human: honest men have done the same before you. But afterwards, did you give it a thought? Or did you look ahead at all and think what you should do and how to do it? If you were ashamed to confess, how was I to find out? You delayed and did nothing while nine months went by. This was the greatest wrong you could do, to yourself, to that poor girl, and the child. Well: did you think you could leave everything to the gods and go on dreaming? And that she would be brought to you as a bride without your stirring a finger? I trust you are not so thoughtless in all your personal affairs. [*Changing his tone, after a pause*] Cheer up, you shall marry her.

AESCHINUS: What?

MICIO: I said, Cheer up.

AESCHINUS: Father, for pity's sake, are you making fun of me now?

MICIO: No, I'm not. Why should I?

AESCHINUS: I don't know, except that I'm so desperately anxious for this to be true that I'm afraid it isn't.

MICIO: Go indoors, and pray the gods to help you bring home your wife. Off with you.

AESCHINUS: What? My wife? Will it be soon?

MICIO: Yes.

AESCHINUS: How soon?

MICIO: As soon as possible.

AESCHINUS [*hugging him*]: Damn me, father, if I don't love you more than my own eyes!

MICIO [*gently disengaging himself*]: What, more than – her?

AESCHINUS: Well, just as much.

MICIO [*ironically*]: Very kind of you.

AESCHINUS [*suddenly remembering*]: But where's that man from Miletus?

MICIO [*airily*]: Lost, gone, on board his ship. . . . *Now* what's stopping you?

AESCHINUS: Father, you go, you pray to the gods. They'll be more likely to listen to you, I know; you're so much better than I.

MICIO: I *am* going in: there are preparations to be made. You be sensible and do what I say. [*He goes into* MICIO'S *house.*]

AESCHINUS [*coming forward*]: What do you think of that? Is this what it means to be a father or a son? A brother or a friend couldn't do more for me. Oh, he's a man to love and cherish in one's heart! If he can be so kind I'll be sure never to be foolish again or do anything he doesn't like. This lesson will be a warning. But I must hurry indoors or I shall delay my own wedding! [*He goes into* MICIO'S *house, and almost at once* DEMEA *comes on wearily, back from his search.*]

DEMEA: I've walked and walked till I'm worn out. Curse you, Syrus, and your directions! I trailed all over the town, to the gate and the pool and everywhere, and found no sign of a workshop at all nor a soul who said he'd seen my brother. Well, my mind is made up: I'm sitting down here outside his house to wait till he comes back.

[MICIO *comes out of his house talking to* AESCHINUS *inside.*]

MICIO: I'll go across and tell them we are all ready now.

DEMEA: Here he is. I've been looking for you for hours, Micio.

MICIO: What for?

DEMEA: I've more news for you: more wicked deeds of that good young man of yours.

MICIO: What, again!

DEMEA: Fresh crimes, awful ones!

MICIO [*impatiently*]: That'll do.

DEMEA: You've no idea of what he is –

MICIO: Yes I have.

DEMEA [*in a fury*]: You fool, you imagine I'm talking about that music-girl; this time it's an honest girl who is Athenian born.

MICIO [*quietly*]: I know.

DEMEA: You *know*? And you allow it?

MICIO: Why shouldn't I?

DEMEA: How can you be so calm? Aren't you furious?

MICIO: No. It's true I should prefer –

DEMEA: And now there's a child.

MICIO [*sincerely*]: Heaven bless it!

DEMEA: The girl has nothing –

MICIO: So I heard.

DEMEA: She'll have to be married without a dowry –

MICIO: I suppose so.

DEMEA: What's to be done now?

MICIO: What the situation requires. She shall be moved from that house to this [*pointing to* SOSTRATA'S *house and his own*].

DEMEA: Good God! Is that the proper thing to do?

MICIO: What more *can* I do?

DEMEA: What indeed! If you really have no feelings about all this, it would surely be only human to *pretend* you have.

MICIO: But I've arranged for him to marry the girl; everything is settled and the wedding is on the way; I've removed their fears for the future; that is what seems to me only human.

DEMEA [*thoughtfully, after a pause*]: But are you really pleased, Micio, with what you've done?

MICIO: If I could alter the situation – no. But as things are, I can't; so I must accept it quietly. Life is like a game of dice; if you don't get the throw you need most, you must use skill to make the best of what turns up.

DEMEA [*furious again*]: Make the best indeed! And this skill of yours has thrown away good money on that music-girl! now she'll have to be sold for what she'll fetch, or given away if no one makes an offer.

MICIO: No; I have no intention of selling her.

DEMEA: Then what *do* you propose to do?

MICIO: She shall stay with us.

DEMEA: Heavens above, is he going to keep a mistress in the same house as his wife?

MICIO: Why not?

DEMEA: Are you really in your right mind?

MICIO: *I* think so.

DEMEA [*with heavy sarcasm*]: Heaven help me, all this tom-foolery makes me wonder if your idea is to have this girl to partner your own singing.

MICIO: Perhaps it is.

DEMEA: And the new bride to join in!

MICIO: Of course.

DEMEA: The three of you dancing hand-in-hand –

MICIO: Certainly.

DEMEA: Certainly?

MICIO [*seizing him by the hand*]: With you to make a fourth if we want one!

DEMEA [*shaking himself free with a cry of disgust*]: Have you no sense of shame?

MICIO [*suddenly serious*]: Now then, Demea, that's enough of your ill-temper. Your son is to be married; can't you be-

have properly? Try to be pleased and look happy. I'm
going to call them; then I'll be back.

[*He goes into* SOSTRATA'S *house*.]

DEMEA: Ye gods, what a life! what morals! what madness!
Here's a bride coming without a penny, and a kept woman
in the house! Too much money in the home, a young man
ruined by indulgence, and the old one off his head! Provi-
dence itself might step in, but this household's beyond
saving!

[SYRUS *staggers out of* MICIO'S *house, drunk and self-
satisfied. He does not see* DEMEA.]

SYRUS: Well, Syrus my lad, you've done yourself proud!
Done your duty handsome-ly. [*Hiccups*] That's better. I've
had all I can take *inside*, so I just took a fancy to stretch my
legs out here. . . .

DEMEA: Now look at that! A fine example of discipline in
the home!

SYRUS [*lurching towards him*]: Why, here's our old man! How
do? Feeling glum?

DEMEA: Scoundrel!

SYRUS: You spouting here now, Father Wisdom?

DEMEA: If you were in my service –

SYRUS: You'd be a rich man to be sure! You'd have a fortune
on a *firm* footing – [*staggers*].

DEMEA: – I would make you an example to all.

SYRUS: Why on earth? What have *I* done?

DEMEA: Done? Here's all this trouble and dreadful wrong-
doing, and nothing properly settled yet, and all you can
do is drink, you wretch, as if there was something to
celebrate.

SYRUS [*somewhat dashed*]: Sorry now I came out. . . .

[DROMO *opens the door of* MICIO'S *house to call* SYRUS.]

DROMO: Hey, Syrus, Ctesipho wants you.

SYRUS [*sufficiently sobered to act promptly, pushes him in again*]:
  Shut up!

DEMEA: What's he saying about Ctesipho?

SYRUS: Nothing.

DEMEA: You brute, is Ctesipho in there?

SYRUS: No, he isn't.

DEMEA: Then why did I hear his name?

SYRUS: It's someone else, a pretty little boy who hangs
  around here. [*Nudging him*] Know him?

DEMEA [*grimly, as he strides towards the door*]: I shall soon find
  out.

SYRUS [*catching at him*]: What's this? where are you going?

DEMEA: Let me go!

SYRUS: You're not going in there!

DEMEA: Keep your hands off me, you swine, unless you
  want me to knock your brains out! [*He dashes into* MICIO'S
  house.]

SYRUS: He's gone . . . and a damned unwelcome visitor he'll
  be, especially to Ctesipho. Now what shall *I* do? Best wait
  for all this to-do to settle down and find a quiet corner to
  sleep off this drop I've taken. That's the idea. [*He staggers off
  right. Soon afterwards* MICIO *comes out of* SOSTRATA'S *house.*]

MICIO: Everything's ready on our side, as I said, Sostrata.
  When you want. . . . What on earth is that banging on my
  door?

  [DEMEA *bursts out.*]

DEMEA: Good God, what can I do? How can I deal with this?
  Shame and sorrow, what can I say? Heaven and earth,
  great Neptune's ocean!

MICIO: Just look at that; no wonder he's shouting, he's found
  it all out. We're done for, the battle's on, and I'll have to
  see what I can do.

DEMEA: Here he comes! You corrupter of both our sons!

MICIO: Kindly control your temper. Calm yourself, Demea.

DEMEA: I *am* controlled, I *am* calm. I won't say another word. Let's face facts. Wasn't it agreed between us (and it was your suggestion, Micio) that you'd not worry about my boy and I'd not worry about yours? Answer me that.

MICIO: It was, I don't deny it.

DEMEA: Then why is my boy drinking in your house? Why keep him there? Why buy him a mistress? Haven't I a right to expect fair play, Micio? What do you want from me? I'm not worrying about your boy, so you leave mine alone.

MICIO: Now you're not being fair –

DEMEA: What!

MICIO: There's an old proverb that friends have everything in common.

DEMEA: Witty, aren't you. Isn't it rather late in the day for that sort of talk?

MICIO: Just listen to me a minute, Demea, if you've no objection. First of all, if it's the money the boys spend which is worrying you, please try to look at it this way. At one time you were bringing up both your sons according to your means, because you thought you would have enough for two, and I suppose at the time you expected me to marry. Very well, keep to your original plan; hoard, scrape, and save to have as much as possible to leave them. You can see merit in that: all right. My money is something they didn't expect, so let them enjoy it. Your capital won't be touched, and anything I add can be counted as something extra. If only you would be willing to see this in a true light, Demea, you'd save yourself and me and the boys a great deal of trouble.

DEMEA: I'm not talking about money. It's their morals, both of them –

MICIO: Wait. I know, I was coming to that. There are a lot of traits in people which are open to discussion. Two men often do the same thing and you might say that one can safely be allowed to do it while the other might not. The difference is not in the thing done but in the doer. I can see signs in these boys which make me confident they will turn out as we want them. I see good sense, intelligence, proper modesty, and mutual affection, and we can be sure they are open and generous in heart and mind. You can call them back to the right path any day you like. You may say you are anxious for them not to be so careless about money, but, my dear Demea, you must realize that in every other respect we grow wiser with increasing years, but the besetting fault of old age is simply this: we all think too much of money. Time will develop this in them well enough.

DEMEA: Be careful, Micio: these fine-sounding arguments and easy ways of yours may destroy us all.

MICIO: No, no, impossible. Come along now, try to listen to me and stop worrying.

DEMEA: As things are I suppose I'll have to. . . . But tomorrow morning at crack of dawn I'm taking my boy away from here to the farm.

MICIO [*humouring him*]: *Before* dawn, I dare say. Only make yourself agreeable for today.

DEMEA: And that girl will have to come too.

MICIO: That'll do the trick! The best way of tying him down. Only mind you keep *her* there.

DEMEA: I'll see to that. Once she's there I'll have her cooking and grinding corn till she's covered with ash and grime and flour, and then I'll send her out gleaning in the midday sun to make her black and burnt as a cinder!

MICIO [*ironically*]: Good! Now I find you talking sense. Go

on: 'And then I'll force my son whatever he says to sleep
with her – '

DEMEA: All right, laugh at me. You're lucky to be in the
mood. I have my feelings. . . .

MICIO: Now don't start again –

DEMEA: No, I've done.

MICIO: Come in then, and spend this day with us in the
proper way.

[*They go into* MICIO'S *house. After a short interval* DEMEA
reappears, much smartened up and perhaps wearing some of
MICIO'S *clothes.*]

DEMEA: A plan for life may be well worked out, but a man
can still learn something new from circumstances, age, and
experience. You find you don't know what you thought
you did, and things which seemed so important before,
you reject in practice. This is what has just happened to me,
for I've lived a hard life up to this very moment and now
I'm giving up when the race is almost won. And why?
Hard facts have shown me that a man gains most from
tolerance and good nature. Look at my brother and me if
you want to see the truth of this. He has always led a life of
leisure, sociable, easy-going, and tolerant, with never a
black look for anyone and a smile for all. He's lived for
himself and spent on himself, and he's won praise and
affection from the whole world. I'm the country bumpkin,
mannerless and surly, truculent, mean and close-fisted, and
when I took a wife what troubles I brought on myself!
Two sons were born – more worry. Thinking of them and
struggling to make all I could for them, see how I've
wasted my youth and my life in money-grubbing! Now
I'm old, and what's my reward for all my trouble? They
don't like me. It's my brother who enjoys the benefits of
fatherhood without having lifted a finger. They love him

and avoid me. He has their confidence and their affection, the two of them are always with him and I'm left all alone. They offer prayers for his long life, but you may be sure they're counting the days for me to die. I've toiled and slaved to bring them up, but he has made them his own for next to nothing, so he has all the enjoyment while the trouble's left to me. Very well then, two can play at that game; let's see now whether I can take up his challenge and show myself capable of soft answers and winning ways! *I* could also do with a bit of love and appreciation from my own children. If that comes from being generous and agreeable, I can take the lead all right. The money may give out, but that needn't worry me – I'm old enough for it to last *my* time.

[SYRUS *comes out of* MICIO'S *house.*]

SYRUS: Please, Sir, your brother hopes you're not leaving us.

DEMEA [*genially*]: Who's that? Ah, Syrus, my man, good evening. How are you and how are things going?

SYRUS: All right, Sir.

DEMEA: Splendid. [*Aside*] That's three things already which aren't like me, 'my man', 'how are you', and 'how are things going'. [*Aloud*] You may be a slave, but you have your finer points, and I should be pleased to do you a good turn.

SYRUS [*incredulous*]: Thank you, Sir.

DEMEA: But I mean it, Syrus, as you'll soon see.

[SYRUS *goes back into the house and* GETA *comes out of* SOSTRATA'S.]

GETA [*to* SOSTRATA]: I'm just going next door, Madam, to see how soon they want the bride. Why, here's Demea. Good evening, Sir.

DEMEA: Let me see now, what's your name?

GETA: Geta, Sir.

DEMEA: Geta, today has convinced me that you are a most valuable person. Nothing recommends a slave to me so much as his care for his master's interests, such as I have seen in you. For this, if the opportunity arises, I should be glad to do you a good turn. [*Aside*] I think my affability improves with practice.

GETA [*puzzled*]: It's kind of you to think so, Sir.

DEMEA [*aside*]: I've made a start, winning over the masses one by one.

[AESCHINUS *and* SYRUS *come out of* MICIO'S.]

AESCHINUS: They're killing me with all their fuss over wedding ceremonies! Here's a whole day wasted with preparations.

DEMEA: What's the matter, Aeschinus?

AESCHINUS: Hullo, father, I didn't know you were there.

DEMEA: Father, yes, in heart and soul, your father who loves you more than his own eyes. But why don't you bring your wife home?

AESCHINUS: That's just what I *want* to do. I'm kept waiting for the flutes and the choir for the marriage-hymn.

DEMEA: Will you take a word of advice from your old father?

AESCHINUS: What is it?

DEMEA: Scrap the lot – flutes, torches, singing, and company – knock a hole in the garden wall here and now and take her across that way, join the two houses and bring the whole lot of them, mother and all, over to us!

AESCHINUS [*hugging him*]: Father, you're simply splendid!

DEMEA [*aside*]: Good, now I'm splendid! Micio'll have to keep open house, with all these people to entertain and no end of expense, but what do I care? I'm splendid and popular! That Croesus can pay out two thousand on the spot. Syrus, what are you waiting for?

SYRUS: What am I to do, Sir?

DEMEA: Knock down the wall. Geta, you go and fetch them.

GETA: Heaven bless you, Sir, for your kindness to us all.

DEMEA: It's no more than you deserve. [GETA *and* SYRUS *go in.*] What do you say?

AESCHINUS [*somewhat bewildered*]: I agree.

DEMEA: She's scarcely up yet after having the baby – much better bring her that way than through the street [*banging and hammering are heard*].

AESCHINUS: Nothing could be better, father.

DEMEA [*smugly*]: Ah, it's just my way. . . . But look, here's Micio.

   [MICIO *bursts out of his house.*]

MICIO: My brother's orders? Where is he? *Are* these your orders, Demea?

DEMEA [*impressively*]: They are. In this and every other way we should unite with this family to cherish and support it and make it one with ours.

AESCHINUS: Yes, please, father.

MICIO [*reluctantly*]: I suppose I have to agree.

DEMEA: Believe me, it's our duty. And now, to start with, this boy's wife has a mother.

MICIO: I know; what of it?

DEMEA: She is virtuous and discreet.

MICIO: So I'm told.

DEMEA: Not too young –

MICIO: I know.

DEMEA: But long since past the age to have children, and with no one to look after her. She's alone. . . .

MICIO: What's the point of all this?

DEMEA: The proper thing for you to do is to marry her. Aeschinus, you persuade him.

MICIO: *I* marry?

DEMEA: You.

MICIO: Did you say *I* should marry her?

DEMEA: I did.

MICIO: You're joking.

DEMEA [*to* AESCHINUS]: Talk to him as man to man and he'll do it.

AESCHINUS: Father –

MICIO: You silly ass, must you listen to him?

DEMEA: It's no good, Micio, you'll have to give in.

MICIO: You're crazy.

AESCHINUS: Do it for my sake, father.

MICIO: You're mad, leave me alone.

DEMEA: Come, do as your son asks.

MICIO: You're off your head. I'm sixty-five: do you propose that I should embark on matrimony with this decrepit old hag for a wife?

AESCHINUS: Come on: I've promised them.

MICIO: *Promised* them? Kindly restrict your generosity to your own person, my dear child.

DEMEA: But he might be asking more of you. . . .

MICIO: There couldn't be anything more.

DEMEA: Do it for him –

AESCHINUS: Don't be difficult –

DEMEA: Come, promise.

MICIO: Leave me alone, can't you!

AESCHINUS: Not until you'll give in.

MICIO: It's an insult!

DEMEA: Now be generous, Micio.

MICIO: This is monstrous, crazy, ludicrous, entirely unsuitable to my whole way of life . . . but if you are both so set on it . . . all right.

AESCHINUS: Well done! You deserve all my love now.

DEMEA: But – [*aside*] I must think up something else now I've won that point.

MICIO: Now what is it?

DEMEA: There's Hegio, their closest relative, who'll be a connexion of ours. He's a poor man, and we ought to do something for him.

MICIO: Well, what?

DEMEA: There's that little bit of property just outside the town which you're always letting out. We can give it to him and he'll make good use of it.

MICIO: Do you call that a 'little bit'?

DEMEA: Big or little, it's what we must do. He has been a father to the girl, he's a good man and one of us, so he ought to have it. After all, I'm only appropriating the sentiment you expressed just now, Micio: 'the besetting fault of us all is that in old age we think too much of money'. Wise words and well put! We must rid ourselves of this defect, and put the truth in this saying into practice.

MICIO [drily]: I'm glad to hear it. Very well. Hegio shall have it when Aeschinus likes.

AESCHINUS: Thank you, father.

DEMEA: Now you are my true brother, body and soul! [aside] And I've got his own knife at his throat!

[SYRUS comes out of the house, dusting himself down.]

SYRUS: Your orders have been carried out, Sir.

DEMEA: Good man. And now I should like to propose that this very day Syrus should receive his freedom.

MICIO: His freedom? Him? Whatever for?

DEMEA: For lots of reasons.

SYRUS [eagerly]: Oh, master, you're a fine gentleman, Sir, indeed you are. I've looked after both the young masters since they were boys, cared for them, taught them, guided them, always given them the best advice I could. . . .

DEMEA [drily]: So I see. And there are other things besides – bargain hunting, procuring a girl, putting on a dinner-party at all hours. It needs no ordinary man to perform services like *these*.

SYRUS: Sir, you're really splendid!

DEMEA: To crown all, it was he who helped us to buy the music-girl; in fact, he arranged it all. He ought to get something for it, and it will have a good effect on the others. . . . And then, Aeschinus wants it.

MICIO: Do you, Aeschinus?

AESCHINUS: Yes, very much.

MICIO: Well, if you really want it – Syrus, come here. [*With a blow*] Take your freedom.

SYRUS [*rubbing himself ruefully*]: You're very kind. I'm grateful to you all, especially you, Sir [*to* DEMEA].

DEMEA: My congratulations.

AESCHINUS: And mine.

SYRUS: Thank you. I believe you. Now there's just one thing to complete my happiness. . . . If only I could see my wife, Phrygia, freed as well!

DEMEA: A very fine woman.

SYRUS: And she was the first, Sir, to come forward as wet-nurse for your grandson, the young master's son, this very day –

DEMEA: Ah, that's a serious reason. If she was the first, she certainly ought to have her freedom.

MICIO: Just for that?

DEMEA: Why not? I'll pay you her value to settle it.

SYRUS: Oh, Sir, heaven always grant you all your wishes!

MICIO: Well, Syrus, you've done pretty well for yourself today.

DEMEA: He has, if you'll carry on with your duty and give him a little something in hand to live on. He'll soon pay you back.

MICIO [*snapping his fingers*]: That's all he'll get.

DEMEA: He's a good fellow.

SYRUS: I'll pay it back, Sir, I promise you, just give me —

AESCHINUS: Come on, father.

MICIO: I'll think about it.

DEMEA [*to* AESCHINUS]: He'll do it.

SYRUS: You're wonderful, Sir!

AESCHINUS: Father, you're a darling!

MICIO: What *is* all this? Why this sudden change of heart? What's the idea of this sudden outburst of generosity?

DEMEA: I'll tell you. I wanted to show you, Micio, that what our boys thought was your good nature and charm didn't come from a way of living which was sincere or right or good, but from your weakness, indulgence, and extravagance. Now, Aeschinus, if you and your brother dislike my ways because I won't humour you in all your wishes, right or wrong, I wash my hands of you — you can spend and squander and do whatever you like. On the other hand, being young, you are short-sighted, over-eager, and heedless, and you may like a word of advice or reproof from me on occasion, as well as my backing at the proper time. Well, I'm here at your service.

AESCHINUS: We'd like that, father. You know best. But what's going to happen to Ctesipho?

DEMEA: I've given my consent; he can keep his girl. But she must be his last.

MICIO: Well done, Demea.

[*They all go into* MICIO'S *house.*]

APPENDIX
'THE LIFE OF P. TERENTIUS AFER' BY
C. SUETONIUS TRANQUILLUS

This is one of the surviving Lives of Famous Men *by the author of* The Twelve Caesars. *It is preserved in the preface to his commentary on the plays of Terence by the fourth-century grammarian, Aelius Donatus, with a short addition of his own.*

Publius Terentius Afer was born at Carthage and was the slave in Rome of the senator Terentius Lucanus, by whom, on account of his intelligence and good looks, he was given not only a gentleman's education but soon afterwards his freedom. Some people believe he was a prisoner of war, but Fenestella [1] says this is impossible, since the dates of his birth and death both fall between the end of the Second Punic War and the beginning of the Third. Again, if he had been captured by the Numidians or Gaetulians, he could not have come into the possession of a Roman master, as there was no trade between Italy and North Africa until after the destruction of Carthage. In Rome he lived on familiar terms with several noble friends, notably Scipio Africanus the Younger and Gaius Laelius, who, it is thought, were attracted by his personal beauty. This, too, Fenestella disproves on the grounds that Terence was older than either of them; though Nepos [2] declares that they were all much the same age, and the following lines of Porcius [3] imply that there was something scandalous in their relationship: 'While he courted the wanton nobility and their dubious

1. The antiquarian and historian of Rome: ?52 B.C.–?19 A.D.
2. Cornelius Nepos, the biographer: ?99–?24 B.C.
3. Porcius Licinus, a poet of the later second century B.C.; this attack on Terence is practically all that survives of his work.

admiration, drank in the godlike voice of Africanus with greedy ears, fancied himself as a frequent diner-out with Philus and handsome Laelius, and was carried off to their Alban estates on account of his youthful beauty, he neglected his own affairs and was reduced to utter poverty. So he fled from men's sight to the far land of Greece, and there he died, at Stymphalia, a town in Arcadia. Thus he gained nothing from Scipio, Laelius, and Furius, who were easily the three greatest noblemen of their day. They gave him no help, not even a house where he could live and keep a servant to report his death.'

He wrote six comedies. When he offered the aediles the first of these, *The Woman of Andros*, he was told he should first read it aloud to Caecilius.¹ He arrived when Caecilius was at dinner, and because he was shabbily dressed he was made to read the opening sitting on a stool by Caecilius' couch. After a few lines he was invited to take a place by Caecilius, and when the meal was over he finished the reading, to Caecilius' great admiration. With this and his five other plays he won fame, though Volcacius² in listing them has said that 'The sixth, *The Mother-in-Law*, must be excepted, as a poor play.' *The Eunuch* was, in fact, twice presented, and won 8,000 sesterces, the highest fee ever paid for a comedy. The sum is recorded on the title-page.

³... for Varro even preferred the beginning of *The Brothers* to the original by Menander. It is generally believed that Terence was helped in his writing by Laelius and Scipio, a rumour which he helped to spread himself by his half-hearted

---

1. Caecilius Statius, Rome's chief comic dramatist after Plautus. Forty-two titles of his plays survive. As he died in 168 B.C. and the *Andria* was first performed in 166, this is not a very probable story.

2. Volcacius Sedigitus, who lived around 100 B.C., wrote in verse on the 'Ten Best Writers of Comedy'. Caecilius heads the list, Plautus comes second, and Terence is sixth.

3. There is a gap in the MS. here.

efforts in rebutting it; for example, in the preface to *The Brothers*: 'As to the spiteful accusation that eminent persons assist the author and collaborate closely with him; his accusers may think it a grave charge, but he takes it as a high compliment if he can win the approval of men who themselves find favour with you all and with the general public, men whose services in peace, in war, and in your private affairs are given at the right moment, without ostentation, to benefit each one of you' (lines 15–21; p. 132).

This half-heartedness in defending himself seems to have been due to his thinking that the idea would please Laelius and Scipio; so the rumour gained ground and has persisted down to later times. In a speech for his own defence Gaius Memmius mentions that Scipio borrowed a character which Terence had acted himself in Scipio's house and put it on the stage in Terence's name; and Nepos relates how he had heard on good authority that while Laelius was staying at his house at Puteoli one first of March, he was asked by his wife to be a little more punctual at dinner. He begged her not to interrupt him, and finally came late into the dining-room remarking that he had not often been so successful in his writing. When asked what he had written, he quoted from *The Self Tormentor*: 'Damn it, Syrus has brought me here pretty impudently with his promises.'[1]

Santra[2] takes the view that if Terence had needed help in his writing he would not have made use of Scipio and Laelius, who were then far too young, but of C. Sulpicius Gallus, a man of learning in whose consulship Terence had first produced a play at the Megalesian Games, or of Q. Fabius Labeo and M. Popillius, both dramatists and men of

1. Line 723. There seems nothing special about this except its skilful use of alliteration (*Sati' pol proterve me Syri promissa huc induxerunt*).
2. A grammarian and literary historian of the later Republic.

consular rank. That is why Terence does not refer to those said to have helped him as *young* men, but as 'men whose services in peace, in war, and in private affairs are given to the people'.

He was not yet twenty-five when he left Rome, after bringing out his comedies, either to get away from the rumour that he was passing off other peoples' work as his own, or to study the institutions and customs of the Greeks which he had not always represented accurately in his plays. He never returned. Volcacius gives this account of his death: 'But when Terence had brought out six comedies he went on a journey to Asia Minor. After he embarked on shipboard he was never seen again, and so his life came to an end.' Cosconius [1] says that he died at sea on the return voyage from Greece bringing new adaptations of Menander, while others relate that he died in Arcadia or Leucadia, in the consulship of Cn. Cornelius Dolabella and M. Fulvius Nobilior, after an illness brought on by grief at the loss of his luggage sent on by sea which contained the new plays he had written.

He is described as being of average height, slight build, and dark complexion. He left a daughter, who subsequently married a Roman knight, and property of twenty *jugera* by the Appian Way, near the Temple of Mars. This makes it all the harder to believe Porcius' statement that 'he gained nothing from Scipio, Laelius, and Furius, who were easily the three greatest noblemen of their day. They gave him no help, not even a house where he could live and keep a servant to report his death.' Afranius,[2] in his *Compitalia*, rates him above all other writers of comedy ('As for Terence, you will not find his like'), but Volcacius puts him lower than

1. A grammarian and writer on law of the first century A.D.
2. Lucius Afranius, born about 150 B.C., was a prolific composer of the *fabulae togatae* portraying Italian domestic life.

Naevius, Plautus, and Caecilius, and even than Licinius and Atilius.

Cicero pays him this tribute in his *Limo*: 'You too, Terence, who alone could command the words to put Menander in our midst, translated and set out in the Latin tongue, his passions spent; whose style can charm, whose every word delights.' Caesar also says: 'You too will take your place on the heights, O half-size Menander, and rightly, as a lover of pure speech. If only your even measures had been endowed with vigour, so that your gift for comedy could be valued as highly as the Greeks', and your works were not lying neglected! This is my great regret, Terence, my sorrow for your loss.'

(Postscript by Aelius Donatus)

This *Life* is by Suetonius Tranquillus. Maccius says there were two poets of the name, Terentius Libo of Fregellae, and the freedman Terence, born an African, the subject of the *Life*. Vagellius [1] argues that Scipio was the author of the plays produced by Terence: 'The plays which are called yours, Terence, whose are they really? Wasn't it our great lawgiver and honoured citizen who wrote them?' Two of the plays are said to have been translated from the comedies of Apollodorus (*Phormio* and *The Mother-in-Law*),[2] and the other four from Menander. *The Eunuch* had great success and won a high fee, while *The Mother-in-Law* failed several times before it was finally successfully staged.

1. A poet of the time of Nero and friend of Seneca.
2. Menander is given as the original in the Production Notice.

BIBLIOGRAPHY

Beare, Wm., *The Roman Stage* (2nd edition, 1955).

Bieber, M., *The History of the Greek and Roman Theater* (2nd edition, 1961).

Bolgar, R. R., *The Classical Heritage* (1954).

Chassang, A., *Des Essais dramatiques imités de l'Antiquité* (1852).

Diderot, D., *Réflexions sur Térence* (1762).

Duckworth, G. E., *The Nature of Roman Comedy* (1951).

Frank, Tenney, *Life and Literature in the Roman Republic* (1930).

Graves, R., Echard's Translation (1689) of *The Comedies of Terence* (1963).

Highet, G., *The Classical Tradition* (1949).

Lawton, H. W., *Térence en France en XVIe siècle* (1926).

Marouzeau, J., *Térence, texte établi et traduit* (Budé edition, 1947).

Meredith, G., *An Essay on Comedy* (1877).

Norwood, G., *The Art of Terence* (1923).

Sainte Beuve, *Nouveaux Lundis* (3 and 10 August 1863).

Sandys, J. E., *A History of Classical Scholarship* (1903).

Sargeaunt, J., *Annals of Westminster School* (1898).

Sargeaunt, J., *The Plays of Terence* (Loeb edition, 1912).

Sellar, W. Y., *Roman Poets of the Republic* (1889).

*A list of the most recent
volumes in the Penguin Classics
is given overleaf*

The most recent volumes in the Penguin Classics are:

EUSEBIUS
History of the Church · *G. A. Williamson*

TURGENEV
Fathers and Sons · *Rosemary Edmonds*

THE VINLAND SAGAS
The Norse Discovery of America · *M. Magnusson
and H. Pálsson*

IBSEN
A Doll's House and Other Plays · *Peter Watts*

LIVES OF THE SAINTS
J. F. Webb

LIVY
The War with Hannibal · *Aubrey de Sélincourt*

BALZAC
Poor Relations, Part 1: Cousin Bette · *Marion Ayton Crawfo*

de MAUPASSANT
A Woman's Life · *H. N. P. Sloman*

ARISTOTLE, HORACE, LONGINUS
Classical Literary Criticism · *T. S. Dorsch*

PLAUTUS
The Pot of Gold and Other Plays · *E. F. Watling*

*For a complete list of books available please write to Penguin Books
whose address can be found on the back of the title page*